CONTENTS

List of Maps	iv
Preface	1
Introduction	3
A. The Papyri	3
B. Work on the *Hellenica Oxyrhynchia*	7
C. Background to the periods covered	16
D. The *Hellenica Oxyrhynchia* as literature	21
Bibliography	23
The *Hellenica Oxyrhynchia*	
Cairo Fragments	29
Florence Fragments	35
London Fragments	45
Commentary	116

LIST OF MAPS

Ephesus   119

Notium, Ephesus and Clazomenae   128

Rhodes and the Carian and Lycian coast   139

The Sardis Campaign, 395 B.C.   142

Electoral divisions of Boeotia   156

Locris, Phocis and Boeotia   168

Agesilaus' march inland   176

HELLENICA

OXYRHYNCHIA

edited with translation and commentary by

P. R. McKechnie & S. J. Kern

© P.R. McKechnie & S.J. Kern 1988. All rights reserved. No part of this publication may be reproduced, stored in a retrieval system, or transmitted in any form by any means without the prior written permission of the publishers. The Greek text of the Cairo fragment was first published in the *Studia Papyrologica* of 1976 and is present in this volume with the kind permission of the Pontifico Istituto Biblico. The Greek text of the fragments in Florence and London is from V. Bartoletti's edition of 1959 and is reproduced here with the kind permission of BSB B.G. Teubner Verlagsgesellschaft (Leipzig).

 British Library Cataloguing in Publication Data

Hellenica Oxyrhynchia. — (Classical texts).
 1. Greece — History — to 146 B.C.
 I. McKechnie, P.R.   II. Kern, S.J.
 III. Series
 938'.06   DF214

ISBN 0 85668 357 4 *cloth*
ISBN 0 85668 358 2 *limp*

Classical Texts ISSN 0953—7961

Cover illustration shows part of Papyrus PSI 1304 and is reproduced with the kind permission of the Istituto Papirologico «G. Vitelli», Florence.

Printed and published in England by:
Aris & Phillips Ltd, Teddington House, Church Street, Warminster, Wiltshire, BA12 8PQ, England.

Preface

The *Hellenica Oxyrhynchia* is one of the most valuable discoveries among literary papyri from Egypt. It deals with the history of Athens and Greece in the late fifth and early fourth centuries, a widely studied period. It can be compared in point of importance for this period with Aristotle's *Constitution of the Athenians*, also discovered in papyrus.

This makes it surprising that no edition with full English translation has been published, and perhaps still more surprising that editions in Greek have been unavailable except in library collections for some years. We hope this edition with translation and brief commentary will meet a need of scholars and students for this important text.

We have had substantial help from several quarters in preparing this book. Most substantially, we have had the use of earlier authors' work - and the frequent references to I.A.F. Bruce *An Historical Commentary on the Hellenica Oxyrhynchia (Cambridge, 1967)*, which we have abbreviated to 'Bruce' throughout, will illustrate the value of this systematic commentary. We have been glad to be able to reprint the texts of V. Bartoletti (from the Teubner texts series, Leipzig, 1959) and L. Koenen (from *Studia Papyrologica* 15 (1976), pp.39-79); we use an abbreviated *apparatus criticus*.

A number of individuals and institutions have helped us in a direct way. Photographs of papyri have been supplied by the British Library, the Ashmolean Museum and the Istituto Papirologico "G. Vitelli" in the University of Florence. A grant towards the cost of materials was made by the British Academy. An unpublished thesis was given by the University of South Africa. Prof. M.H. Crawford has commented on a large part of the translation and commentary and discussed with us a number of the issues involved. Mrs

L.A. Botha supplied information by correspondence. Mr A.I. Wilson discussed and advised on several points, and at an early stage in the project Prof. D.M. Lewis gave valuable guidance. The general editor of the Aris and Phillips Classified Texts series, Prof. M.M. Willcock, gave encouragement and valuable comment; and Mr P. Mudd and Mr J. Aris, both of Aris and Phillips, have been thoroughly helpful.

The Preface, Introduction and Commentary were produced to camera-ready standards using the laser-printing facility at the Cambridge University Computer Laboratory. We wish to thank Mrs A. Harrison and Ms L. Ball for entering and editing text. Maps were prepared by Mrs J. Lovell and Paul McKechnie.*

We regard ourselves as jointly responsible for the whole work, for whose mistakes and imperfections we are to blame; but Stephen Kern drafted most of the translation (not all) and Paul McKechnie most (but not all) of the Introduction and Commentary. We have generally latinized names.

We should explain that we use Bartoletti's numbering system for the chapters, and have dropped the use of Grenfell and Hunt's chapter numbers: but we have not felt it right to attempt to renumber the whole thing to allow for the Cairo papyrus being earlier in the work than the rest, so it is referred to simply by column and line.

*The index was prepared by Mr. M. Sharp.

Paul McKechnie   The Perse School
Stephen Kern   March 1987

Introduction

A. The Papyri

Since the publication by B.P. Grenfell and A.S. Hunt in *Oxyrhynchus Papyri* V (London, 1908) of the papyrus, found in 1906, which forms the main part of the *Hellenica Oxyrhynchia*, two other papyri have been found containing material which is generally agreed to form part of the work of the author of the main fragment. The three fragments are all from different copies of the same text. They are introduced here in the chronological order of the narrative in them.

1. The Cairo Fragment PCairo   26   6 SR 3049
                                 27   1

The most recently discovered fragment, kept at the Egyptian Museum in Cairo, and first published by L. Koenen in *Studia Papyrologica* 1976, deals with earlier events than the other two. It is also the oldest papyrus. It is a rather dark coloured piece of papyrus in four parts, of which three join and form a document measuring about 21 cm by 17 cm. The fourth fragment is positioned at the bottom of column 1 by reference to the Demotic list of expenditures on the verso of the roll. The letters are small and square (about 2 mm high, except phi, which tends to have a 4-5 mm down stroke), in straight lines with quite wide gaps (3-4 cm) between. The columns are about 7.5 cm wide and more than 19 cm high, with gaps of about 2 cm between columns. Koenen (p. 55) dates the script to the late first century A.D.

2. The Florence Fragment P.S.I. 1304

The other relatively small papyrus, found at Oxyrhynchus in 1934 and kept at the Istituto Papirologico 'G. Vitelli' in the University of Florence, was first published by V. Bartoletti in *Papiri greci e latini* 1949. It deals with events later than those of the Cairo papyrus, but in the same year. There are four fragments of papyrus, mostly light in colour, which do not join. A small fifth fragment joins as part of fragment A. This papyrus has no writing on the verso. Fragment A is 13.7 cm by 15.5 cm; fragment B is 10.7 cm by 20.5 cm; fragment C is 14.5 cm by 10.5 cm and fragment D is 2.4 cm by 3.2 cm. The letters are in a flowing, rather angular style, 2 to 4 mm high in lines less fiercely straight than those of the Cairo papyrus with gaps between lines not usually more than 2 mm. The columns are about 8.8 cm wide and more than 16 cm high, with gaps of 1.7 cm to 2 cm in between. The script is dated to the late second century A.D. by Bartoletti (*Bruce*, p. 2).

3. The London Fragment P.Oxy. 842

The principal papyrus is a much more complex find than the other two. Found in 1906, it consisted at first of about 230 fragments, which were pieced together by Grenfell and Hunt leaving only 57 fragments unplaced. Unlike the other two papyri, the London papyrus has the historical text written on the verso, and the recto has a demotic land-survey register of the Arsinoite nome (P.Oxy. 918). There are twenty-one columns altogether, divided into four groups of fragments A, B, C and D.

A consists of two relatively large pieces of papyrus with two small fragments. The first, with columns 1 and 2, is 23 cm by 21 cm; the second, with columns 3 and 4, is 7 cm by 21 cm. B, columns 5 to 8, consists of a fragment 21 cm by 20.5 cm, and four small fragments. Grenfell and Hunt expressed doubt whether columns 1-4 or 5-8 should be placed first. C is very fragmentary indeed and consists mainly of two pieces, the first 3.5 cm by 17.1 cm and the other 8.2 cm by 7.8 cm; there are also eight small fragments: between them, these account for columns 9 and 10. D is the best preserved and contains columns 11 to 21, which are continuous. There are two pieces, the first 59.3 cm by 20.4 cm, and the second 50.2 cm by 20.4 cm. There are probably columns lost between each of sections A, B, C and D.

In most of the London papyrus the letters are in a clear, slightly forward-sloping style. They are 2-3 mm high with 2-3 mm between lines. Column 5 and column 6 lines 1-26 are in a different hand, smaller and less regular with smaller gaps between lines. Column 5 has 60 lines, while the others have about 40. The columns are about 8.5 cm wide and vary in height between not much over 16 cm and just under 20 cm. The gaps between columns in the work of the main scribe are 1.8 cm to 2 cm. Grenfell and Hunt described the script as 'a transitional stage between the earlier specimens of this style of the late first or early second century and the ordinary third century type' (*Oxyrhynchus Papyri* V, p. 111); internal evidence in the land survey on the recto places it before Commodus became emperor (A.D. 177).

The delta in the left hand margin at column 5 line 45 is probably a stichometrical letter indicating the 400th line copied by a professional scribe. Evidently the government document on the recto was kept for reuse: E.G. Turner describes how officials in Egypt used to keep papyrus to copy (or have copied) texts that interested them (*Greek Papyri* (Oxford, 1968), p. 90). The high value and relative scarcity of papyrus, even in Egypt, meant that literary works were often copied on the backs of other documents.

Factors Connecting the Fragments

Since the three papyri are not parts of the same copy, the hypothesis that they belong together is founded on the connections between their contents. As the Cairo and Florence fragments are both passages from a narrative dealing with 409 B.C. and unrelated to Xenophon's *Hellenica* there is *prima facie* a plausible feel to the idea that they might be from the same book. The London fragment deals with events about fourteen years later but is quite long and allows certain stylistic points and mannerisms to be noticed.

The author of the London fragment writes straightforward fourth century Greek prose. He uses parataxis, and specially the contrasting particles *men* and *de*, very often; he tends to avoid hiatus; and there are no sustained speeches in the extant portion of the work. Koenen, p. 62, notes the use of *tunchanein* plus participle ('*happen to* be such-and-such') in all three texts (twelve instances altogether), and comments on expressions on the pattern of 'the harbour called Coressus' (Cairo papyrus line 12), 'the place called Miletou Teichos' (22.3) and 'the river [called] Cau[nius]' (9.3). This second expression particularly is certainly used so often in chapters 21-22 of the London papyrus as to qualify as a mannerism: 'the plain of Thebe and the one called [Apia]' (21.1); 'Olympus called Mysian' and 'the mercenaries called Dercylidean' (21.2); and 'a place which is called Leonton Cephalae' (21.5).

Some other texts have been mentioned in connection with the *Hellenica Oxyrhynchia*; for example P.Mich. 5982, a single column 6.3 cm by 18.4 cm found in the University of Michigan dig at Karanis in 1930 and dated to the second century A.D. (R. Merkelbach and H.C. Youtie 'Ein Michigan-Papyrus über Theramenes' ZPE 2 (1968), pp. 161-169). It deals with Theramenes' role in surrender negotiations between Athens and Sparta in 404 and has verbal similarities to Lysias 12 (*Eratosthenes*).69. M. Treu ('Einwände gegen die Demokratie in der Literatur des 5./4. Jh.' *Studii Clasice* 12 (1970), pp. 17-31) suggests that the Lysias passage and the papyrus fragment have a common source (pp. 20-21): he goes on to suggest that apparent stylistic differences between the Michigan papyrus and the *Hellenica*

Oxyrhynchia are not sufficient to prevent their being identified as parts of the same text (p. 31). But A. Andrewes' suggestion, that the papyrus is part of a polemical pamphlet responding to what Lysias says about Theramenes in the Eratosthenes speech, gives a more convincing explanation of the verbal similarities ('Lysias and the Theramenes Papyrus' *ZPE* 6 (1970), pp. 35-38: cf. A. Heinrichs 'Zur Interpretation des Michigan-Papyrus über Theramenes' *ZPE* 3 (1969), pp. 101-108).

As fragments of three copies of the *Hellenica Oxyrhynchia* have been found already, it is possible that further portions may be discovered and identified. There is enough material in the sections now available to give the basis for comparison of an item like P.Mich. 5982 with the rest on more than speculative grounds; and with three copies attested in Egypt, it is clear that in the first and second centuries A.D. the *Hellenica Oxyrhynchia* was not an extreme literary rarity.

B. Work on the Hellenica Oxyrhynchia

The original publication of the London fragment of the *Hellenica Oyxrhynchia* in 1908 was greeted with interest, and by 1910 a dozen or so articles on it, or aspects of it, were published in journals. In 1909, as well as Grenfell and Hunt's Oxford Classical Text (including the fragments of Theopompus and Cratippus), E. Meyer's *Theopomps Hellenika* appeared: the text republished with commentary reflecting the weight of Meyer's certainty on the question of authorship.

Assigning an author to the work was from the beginning one of the main aims scholars set themselves. This and the Boeotian Constitution attracted the strongest curiosity at first. Some comparatively recent writers have tended to disparage the preoccupation with authorship (see for instance those cited by Bruce at p. 22 n. 1). Given that eighty years' thought has failed to produce general agreement on the point it is understandable that there should be a feeling that no argument on existing evidence is likely to compensate for the lack of direct attestation. But there is a certain amount that can be said about the author and the nature of his book.

In the first place, it is established with something near certainty that the book was written as a continuation of Thucydides' history. There are several direct indications of this: Thucydides is referred to by name, apparently in a reference back to something in his work (2); the *Hellenica Oxyrhynchia* uses a division of the year into summer and winter (9) like the system used by Thucydides; and the Cairo and Florence fragments deal with a time shortly after the point at which Thucydides' account breaks off. This has immediate consequences: first, that the author is not going to be Ephorus, because Ephorus' work was not planned on nearly such a strict chronological plan as Thucydides', nor related to it as a continuation (cf. G.L. Barber *The Historian Ephorus* (London, 1935), pp. 17-48); second, that a contemporary alternative to Xenophon's view of the narrative of this period is now at any rate partly extant.

Here authorship begins to appear important, particularly since the *Hellenica Oxyrhynchia* is indirectly a main source for Diodorus Siculus, whose first century B.C. account of this period is fully extant. This account was based on Ephorus, who used the *Hellenica Oxyrhynchia* as a source. The commentary notes some of the points at which the *Hellenica Oxyrhynchia*/Diodorus tradition differs from Xenophon's accounts and those of Plutarch, who read Xenophon. The question is typically which version to regard as the fairer picture. Xenophon's biases are well known: he was a rich Athenian soldier, pro-Spartan, anti-democratic. But he lived through the period he wrote about, and had some personal contact with important people and events. While the name and background of the writer who (unknowingly) established the other tradition remain unclear, and it is not known whether the work was written a short or long time after the events it describes, evaluation and comparison are hazardous.

The names of a good many history writers are known. It has been argued, for instance by H. Bloch and G.E. Underhill, that the author of the *Hellenica Oxyrhynchia* is a person not now known by name. This argument is plausible because it is possible to argue against any known name that may be suggested, but it is increasingly unattractive now that as many as three papyrus copies are attested: it must be likely that the history is the work of someone whose name was mentioned by later writers.

Exploration has centred on the names of Theopompus and Cratippus. Grenfell and Hunt titled the London fragment 'Theopompus (or Cratippus) Hellenica' in the *editio princeps*. J.H. Lipsius in 1916 made a rejoinder against E. Meyer's *Theopomps Hellenika* by republishing the text under the Latin title *Cratippi Hellenicorum fragmenta Oxyrhynchia*. These writers, Theopompus and Cratippus, both wrote continuations of Thucydides' work.

Theopompus started at the battle of Cynossema (411/10) and went down to the battle of Cnidus, 17 years later, in twelve books: this is noted by Diodorus at the beginning and end of the period concerned (D.S. XIII.42.5 and XIV.84.7). This timespan would include the extant fragments, placing the Cairo and Florence fragments near the beginning of the work and the London fragment close to the end. Comments by ancient literary critics on Theopompus' work partly encourage identification with the author of the *Hellenica Oxyrhynchia*, but also raise difficulties. The comment in Athenaeus that Theopompus was a lover of truth and spent a great deal of money on accurate fact-finding to do with his history (*FGrHist* 115T28a: Athen. III.85A) could square with the evidently serious nature of the *Hellenica Oxyrhynchia*, and Photius' observation that Theopompus spun out his historical works with many digressions on all sorts of historical matters (*FGrHist* 115T31) could fit in nicely with features like the digression on the Boeotian Constitution (16-17).

The stylistic difficulty is that in antiquity Theopompus was apparently regarded as a rhetorical historian of a rather passionate kind. Cicero talks of his 'high and exalted style' (*Brutus* 66) and Polybius quotes in Theopompus' own words a vivid diatribe, against the courtiers of King Philip of Macedon (VIII.9.6-13: *FGrHist* 115F225c), which is a very carefully worked up rhetorical attack. It has been pointed out, for instance by Bruce (p. 23), that there is nothing of this sort in the *Hellenica Oxyrhynchia*. And Theopompus' work included speeches (*FGrHist* 115F164 and F166), of which the extant part of the Hellenica Oxyrhynchia has none. Another strong argument against Theopompus as author, in some writers' view, is provided by Porphyry's statement in connection with the meeting of Agesilaus and Pharnabazus that Theopompus had changed much of what was in Xenophon's *Hellenica*, and for the worse (*FGrHist* 115T21: cf. Commentary below, p.178).

This is a crucial passage and it is important to understand it. Porphyry, after noting that he has read the *Hellenica* respectively of both Theopompus and Xenophon, and saying that Theopompus has changed them for the worse (he is certainly writing about something he regards as plagiarism), gives a specific example: 'in particular the part about the meeting of Pharnabazus with Agesilaus arranged by Apollophanes of Cyzicus, and the conversations they both had with each other under truce, which Xenophon wrote of in Book IV very pleasingly and suitably: putting this in Book XI of his *Hellenica* Theopompus made it idle and stodgy and useless.' It seems possible (at least to us) from this account that what Porphyry was reading in Theopompus was not an unsuccessful plagiaristic semi-rewrite, but an independent account which lacked the features Porphyry liked in Xenophon (the rather lively conversation which points up the characters of the actors).

The last important difficulty with Theopompus is chronological. He was born in 378/7 (*FGrHist* 115T2: cf. Jacoby's commentary at *FGrHist* IID p. 352). The *Hellenica Oxyrhynchia* was apparently not written before 386 (cf.

Commentary below, p.154). The latest date when it could have been written is less easy to determine - it was done before the Persian Empire fell (it refers in the present tense to the King's way of running the Empire at 19.2) and it says (again in the present tense) that the Phocians have some disputed land near Mount Parnassus (18.3): this places its writing before the fall of Phocis in 346, and it has been suggested that the author did not know of the outbreak of the Sacred War in 356 (Lipsius made this his chief argument against Theopompus' authorship). The second inference is not compelling: it would still make sense to refer to the land as disputed during the decade of intermittent warfare. But if Theopompus is to have written the *Hellenica Oxyrhynchia* he must have been young, and he is hardly likely to have completed the twelve books of his *Hellenica* before about 350. It would mean that the *Hellenica Oxyrhynchia*, though not produced much later than Xenophon's *Hellenica* (which goes down to 362 and began to circulate not much before 356), was produced forty to seventy years after the events it describes, and by a writer who was not yet born when those events happened. But it has its attractions: Theopompus was still looking for his life's work when he finished the *Hellenica* (whether or not it is the *Hellenica Oxyrhynchia*), and he turned afterwards to writing his 58 books of *Philippica*. There is no evidence that he was ever a particularly slow composer.

Cratippus is another matter. Dionysius of Halicarnassus describes him (*De Thucydide* 16) as of the same generation as Thucydides. If he is the author of the *Hellenica Oxyrhynchia* he must have conceived the idea fairly soon after Thucydides' death and finished it within not too many years, before he became too old. It would be in the strict sense contemporary history. There are two possible arguments against the supposition that Cratippus might be the author.

The first is straightforward. As H. Bloch noted ('Studies in Historical Literature of the Fourth Century: I. The Hellenica of Oxyrhynchus and its authorship' *HSCP* Supp. vol. I (1940), pp. 303-341 at p. 313), Dionysius of Halicarnassus also says (*De Thucydide* 9) that no author after Thucydides used his system of dating by the division of the year into summers and winters. The Oxyrhynchus Historian does use this system: so it is possible to argue that Dionysius, who did know Cratippus' work, did not know the *Hellenica Oxyrhynchia*. But there is some danger that deductive rigour of this sort may be misplaced in this instance: the *Hellenica Oxyrhynchia* may have slipped Dionysius' mind, or he may not have meant his statement to be used as an absolutely categorical proposition.

The second argument against Cratippus is less tangible but more radical. There has been doubt about whether Dionysius of Halicarnassus was right to say that Cratippus was of the same generation as Thucydides. F. Jacoby thought the Cratippus note in the *De Thucydide* was a marginal note made by a writer later than Dionysius and later incorporated in the text. He took the view that Cratippus was a writer probably of Hellenistic date, perhaps second century B.C.

This is the sort of thing which is difficult to prove either way. Diodorus mentions only Xenophon and Theopompus as continuators of Thucydides (D.S. XIII.42.5 and XIV.84.7), but Dionysius' statement on Cratippus' date is quite specific and, as P. Pédech observes ('Un historien nommé Cratippe' *REA* 92 (1970), pp. 31-45), stronger arguments would be required to reject it. G.A. Lehmann examines the opening of Plutarch's *De Gloria Atheniensium*, which explicitly acknowledges Cratippus as a source, and aims to compare the emphases and priorities suggested there with those of the *Hellenica Oxyrhynchia* ('Ein Historiker namens Kratippos' *ZPE* (1976), pp. 265-288). He argues for instance that Archinus, mentioned in the *De Gloria Atheniensium* and apparently a top politician, of the Thrasybulus/Anytus rank, from 404 well into the period of the Corinthian War, clearly featured appropriately in Cratippus, and that it is astonishing (if

Cratippus wrote the *Hellenica Oxyrhynchia*) that such an influential politician should not turn up in the *Hellenica Oxyrhynchia* account of the beginning of the Corinthian War (pp. 278-279).

At the heart of Lehmann's argument is the suggestion that Cratippus' work involved a patriotic interpretation of Athenian politics after 404 as involving struggle against Sparta, while other sources give a picture of the restored democracy as initially a loyal subject ally of Sparta (cf. Xen. *Hell.* II.2.20 and 4.38, and Arist. *Ath. Pol.* 39.2): and his conclusion (p. 288) is that Cratippus should be put close to the authors of the Athenian-patriotic Atthidography - not only in terms of outlook but also in point of date (mid-fourth century). He suggests that this view does not bring Dionysius of Halicarnassus' evidence on the dating of Cratippus radically into question. This particular view of Cratippus has the merit that it uses the only extant work known to have been influenced by Cratippus: the extant fragments of Cratippus from other sources amount to very little (*FGrHist* 64), so there is not much scope for making new points for or against Cratippus.

Other names besides Theopompus and Cratippus which have been mentioned as possible authors must be considered outsiders. Androtion the Atthidographer will not have used the dating formulae (years; summers and winters) found in the *Hellenica Oxyrhynchia*: and he (contrary to *Hellenica Oxyrhynchia* 17.5) pictures Attica as badly devastated in the Archidamian War (*FGrHist* 324F39). F. Jacoby's suggestion was Daimachus of Plataea. This is not a well-known name but the idea does not deserve the scorn which has occasionally been poured on it (e.g. A.W. Gomme 'Who was "Kratippos"?' *CQ* n.s. 4 (1954), pp. 53-55). Porphyry does note that Ephorus plagiarized Daimachus (*FGrHist* 65T1a); and as a Plataean Daimachus would be quite well placed to write both the detailed account of the Boeotian Constitution and the comments on Athenian politics which feature in the Oxyrhynchus text. He also wrote a book on siegecraft (*FGrHist* 65T3 and 4), which might be evidence of the sort of interest in stratagems which the Oxyrhynchus Historian had. The extreme dearth of information about Daimachus makes it unlikely that anyone will prove he did not write the *Hellenica Oxyrhynchia* except by showing conclusively which of the other candidates did.

So the question of authorship is not settled. E. Ruschenbusch has traced the uses of three words, of which the first, *antipoliteuesthai* ('to campaign politically against [someone]') was a new coinage of Theopompus (*FGrHist* 115F261) and the others, *meteorizein* and *brabeuein*, were first used metaphorically in Theopompus' time. *antipoliteuesthai* is used only five times in Diodorus, and then in connection with events or persons mentioned by Theopompus (E. Ruschenbusch ('Theopompea: antipoliteuesthai' *ZPE* 39 (1980), pp. 81-90). Ruschenbusch argues that the word cannot have formed part of Ephorus' normal vocabulary (or it would turn up elsewhere in Diodorus) and so was probably copied from Theopompus. Three of the five uses of the word are in connection with the year 409. There is no way of proving that only one writer could have used a particular word, but recent work has tilted the apparent balance of likelihood in favour of Theopompus as author: the question remains open, though.

There is something to be gained from thinking further on the basis of this likelihood. At issue is the relative reliability of Xenophon and the *Hellenica Oxyrhynchia*, and, where the *Hellenica Oxyrhynchia* is involved as indirect source *via* Ephorus, the relative reliability of Xenophon and Diodorus. If, as seems likely, the *Hellenica Oxyrhynchia* was written slightly later than Xenophon's *Hellenica* then it has no claim to enhanced credibility on the basis of being more contemporary with the events it records.

It will be argued in the Commentary that the author in several places shows a bias in favour of the rich: the grounds for thinking his account likely to be less biased than Xenophon's are not *a priori* particularly strong. Next to authorship, the key general question which writers on the *Hellenica*

Oxyrhynchia have had to face is the question of what approach it is best to take to those points where the two traditions differ. There are two lines which can be taken.

The first, and at least up to recent years the commoner of the two, is the line of looking at the accounts where they differ (and more generally) and deciding which carries the more conviction. To twentieth century scholars it is impressive when an account has detail, does not seem overdone and avoids excessive stress on the author's value-judgments. By contrast an account involving a large number of asides on the lines of 'so this seems to me to have been his [Agesilaus'] first fine achievement' (Xen. *Ages.* 1.12, and there is plenty more of this sort of thing) demands cautious handling in a much more obvious way. So for instance A. Andrewes comments on the battle of Notium ('Notion and Cyzicus: the sources compared' *JHS* 102 (1982), pp. 15-25 at p. 18) that 'very considerable weight should be given to the fact that the Oxyrhynchus Historian took the trouble to explain the commanders' intentions ... no later author known to us even considered the possibility that Antiochos had an intelligible plan.' Similarly on the Phrygian campaign C. Dugas ('La Campagne d'Agésilas en Asie Mineure' *BCH* 34 (1910), pp. 58-95 at p. 85) says 'in this account the brevity and dryness of P [the Oxyrhynchus Historian] seems to me closer to the truth than Xenophon's literary and dramatic developments.' Scholars who attach weight to this style of argument tend to find the *Hellenica Oxyrhynchia* in general more convincing than Xenophon.

The second and opposite line of approach is most explicitly explained by V.J. Gray ('Two different approaches to the battle of Sardis in 395 B.C.' *CSCA* 12 (1979), pp. 183-200). She argues (p. 185) that the type of detail in the Oxyrhynchus account is a literary feature of the text: *akribeia* rather than *enargeia* (*accuracy* rather than *clarity*) - the second of which Polybius regards as the mark of a historian familiar with his subject. On the subject of the march to Sardis she comments 'it was sufficient for Xenophon's purpose to have it referred to as the shortest route and leave it at that. If it was the normal route and P still gave a full itinerary, then he would appear to be the sort of historian who believed detail important for its own sake. This was not Xenophon's approach to history.' She notes Xenophon's interest in leadership and shows how the points he uses in his account are chosen on the grounds of relevance to that interest.

This approach makes sympathy for Xenophon's version respectable again. Gray reinforces it in the case of the Sardis march by documenting the *Hellenica Oxyrhynchia*'s tendency to include stratagems[1] and so casting some suspicion on the account of the Sardis ambush. This of course supplies its own counter-argument: if a writer thought stratagems (planning, intellect) relevant they might go in, as the evidences for Agesilaus' personal qualities went into Xenophon's work. The conclusion (and the premiss on which the Commentary in this edition is based) is that there is no substitute for close examination of all possible evidence at each point, and that in some cases there is no resolution possible to points of conflict.

C. Background to the periods covered

1. 409-407

By the middle of the fifth century Athens had become a great power. The Persians, who under Cyrus had come to the fore about 550, had taken

---

[1] p. 196. The stratagems are:
1. Antiochus at Notium (*Hell. Oxy.* 4)
2. Secret messages (5)
3. Sardis ambush (11)
4. Conon's stratagem at Rhodes (15)
5. Theban stratagem to begin war against Sparta (18)
6. Conon's prevention of mutiny at Rhodes (20)
7. Ambush in Mysia (21).
(8.) It is not quite clear, but there may be another strategem at Cairo Fragment col.II.

control of the Median, Lydian, Babylonian and Egyptian kingdoms in the third quarter of the sixth century; but Athens, whose importance in the defeat of the Persian invasion of Greece in 480/79 had not been greater (or not much) than that of Sparta, had taken after the invasion the decisive role in leading the fight against the Persians in the Aegean and Eastern Mediterranean. The Persians had to give up their hopes of controlling the Aegean islands or the Asia Minor seaboard. Athens had tribute and alliance from the states in this area; could coerce states who resisted this control; and established settlements of Athenians (cleruchies) at key points. The Aegean basin, prosperous and militarily advanced (specially at sea) was organized as an empire. The rest of Greece was not.

In 431 the Spartans and their friends began a war against Athens. The first ten years' fighting proved indecisive: success in taking 292 Spartans captive at Pylos in 425 gave Athens hostages against Sparta's annual invasions of Attica, and Brasidas' success in attracting defections from the Athenian Empire in the Thracian area brought about a position whereby both sides more or less wanted the peace treaty of 421. But Sparta's allies, Boeotia and Corinth, were not content with the settlement, and Sparta's old enemy, Argos, was ready to start fighting after the expiry of a thirty-year treaty made in 451. The war went on. In 415 the Athenians decided to send a large expedition and attempt to conquer Sicily. This force was completely destroyed in 413.

Money spent, fleet destroyed, the best of their men dead, the Athenians managed to fight on almost another ten years. Thucydides, who lived through the whole twenty seven years of the war, did not manage to finish writing his history of it. It breaks off in 411, and this is where Xenophon's *Hellenica* begins. The first extant fragment of the *Hellenica Oxyrhynchia* fits in soon after this point. In this period the Spartans captured and fortified Decelea, a place in Attica, and used it as a base for a more systematic programme of damage to property in Athenian territory. But the Athenians were able to secure their seaborne food supply from the Black Sea area by building a new fleet. They stemmed the flow of revolts against them in the Aegean which had begun after their Sicilian defeat.

The Spartans were not likely to win the war, even against a weakened Athens, except by separating the Aegean allies (subject states) from Athens and cutting off the supply of food imports to Athens. An arrangement with the Persians was what Sparta needed: the Persian government, Athens' old enemy, had been antagonized by Athenian support in 414 for Amorges' revolt. Despite Alcibiades' advice not to give decisive support to either side, the Persians agreed to join with Sparta against Athens.

Alcibiades was a flamboyant and talented Athenian who had come to political prominence as an opponent of the peace treaty of 421. Suspicion that he was plotting to overthrow the democratic constitution arose before the Sicilian expedition, and he was recalled to Athens in 415 while he was serving as a general in Sicily; he made himself an exile rather than face trial. After spending some time in Sparta (the idea of occupying Decelea was his) he had been able to attach himself to Tissaphernes, the Persian commander in Western Asia Minor. In 411 the Athenian forces based in Samos voted to allow him to 'return' to them with immunity from prosecution and he promised that by using his influence he would bring the Persian support to Athens instead of Sparta.

In fact Persian support, though sometimes half-hearted, remained with Sparta: but between 411 and 407 Alcibiades led the Athenian forces in the Aegean in a string of successful operations, outstanding among which was the destruction of the Spartan fleet at the battle of Cyzicus in 410, after which the Spartans offered to make peace. The Athenians refused, but welcomed Alcibiades back to Athens itself with great enthusiasm.

The two smaller fragments deal with events in this interlude of optimistic feelings at Athens. The attack on Ephesus was an opportunistic attempt in 409 at getting control of this important city. The skirmish in Megarian territory, though on a small scale, shows the Athenians doing something not achieved since 425 - getting the better of a Spartan land force. And then in 407 the battle of Notium ended this run of success. Alcibiades' fleet was defeated in battle during his own absence: his credibility at Athens was gone for ever - so badly so that when in 405, happening to be in the neighbourhood, he gave some obviously sensible advice to the Athenian admirals at Aegospotami, it was rejected out of hand and the battle lost. With it went the last hope of saving the corn supply and avoiding surrender.

2. 396-394

At the surrender Athens was forced to demolish part (not all) of the long walls between Piraeus and Athens, and to maintain not more than a dozen triremes. The Spartans encouraged the formation of the oligarchy of the Thirty, as elsewhere they set up the dekarchies (ten-man juntas); but in 403 democracy was re-established in Athens. The Spartans, and in particular Lysander, the leading figure in their military successes from 410 onwards, aimed to take Athens' place as hegemonists in the Aegean.

Had it not been for Cyrus the Younger, it is possible that this need not have led to conflict with Persia so soon. He, the son of the King, had arrived to take command in Western Asia Minor in 407 and had become a friend of Lysander. When a brother of his came to the throne as Artaxerxes II in 401, he raised an army with substantial if discreet Spartan support and marched to Babylon to take the kingship for himself. He was killed in battle and his army defeated. Tissaphernes, who had remained loyal to the government, returned to take charge and began military operations against the Greek cities in the west in 400. They appealed to the Spartans to protect them, and Thibron was sent to Asia with an army.

In the London fragment of the *Hellenica Oxyrhynchia* events are moving along two more or less separate lines of development. The Persians are never quite out of the picture. An alliance of Greek states against the Spartans is forming, centring on Boeotia. Dissatisfied in 404 that the Spartans chose not to destroy Athens totally, Boeotia is now governed by people who want combined action, involving a combination of states, to restrict Sparta's power.

The author deals at length with the constitution and political situation in Boeotia; he also documents how the Athenians were divided on the question of how far it was safe to go in taking action against Sparta. For them there was Conon in the background: after serving at Aegospotami he had understandably (in view of the execution in 406 of the Arginusae generals) avoided Athens and gone to Cyprus. By now he was in charge of the fleet which had been built by the Persians in Phoenicia to challenge Spartan naval dominance in the Aegean. So the Persians' strength at sea is increasing while in Greece the Spartans are having plans laid against them.

These are the broad outlines. There is incident. Agesilaus, the King of Sparta, campaigns in Asia with some success: but soon after the time dealt with in the fragments he has to be recalled to fight off the threat to Sparta itself. Conon manoeuvres to see a friendly government installed, to finance his fleet, to quell a mutiny: but soon afterwards he is to defeat the Spartans in a great sea battle, and give the Athenians the protection they need to rebuild their long walls.

Several times in the London fragment the author refers back to events in the Decelean war or even earlier. The issues at stake then have not changed. They concern politics and power. Democracy and oligarchy are often under consideration, if allusively; and the nature of relations between Persia, centrally governed, and the states or groupings of states of the Greeks, is central to the history of the whole period: the end of the Peloponnesian war, which established Sparta as the dominant Greek State, simply added to the complexity of these relations, putting on Sparta some of the interests and constraints to which Athens had formerly been subject.

D. The *Hellenica Oxyrhynchia* as literature

When Thucydides began his history, history-writing was still fairly close to being a new craft. In the middle of the fifth century Herodotus had produced his history: his predecessors in writing narrative prose were lesser authors. A generation later Thucydides found himself a subject as good as Herodotus had had. He brought important new ideas into history writing: he divided up his material by summers and winters; many of the things he wrote about he had first hand knowledge of; and his analysis and interpretation of events was an advance on anything which had gone before.

Thucydides did not live to complete his work. By the time of his death, after the end of the war, his work was at a stage to be attractive to a continuator. Continuing the work of a writer of Thucydides' stature would give a certain imputed authority to the new book. There are two continuations of Thucydides extant: the *Hellenica Oxyrhynchia* and Xenophon's *Hellenica*.

In his *Hellenica* Xenophon covered the years from 411 to 362. But internal evidence suggests that the work may have been produced by stages: the 411 to 404 section shows a more annalistic treatment, and does not include the personal comments which Xenophon incorporates in later parts of the work. In later parts he refers to sacrifices made before and after battle, but in the 411-404 part he uses a more Thucydidean approach and does not include them. The implication of this is that Xenophon probably began his work on the *Hellenica* with the primary intention of completing Thucydides' history: at that point he probably did not have a plan in mind which was anything like the overall shape of the *Hellenica* as it turned out.

Indeed much of the history recorded in the later parts of the *Hellenica* had probably not yet happened when Xenophon began to write his continuation of Thucydides. To some extent this is speculation, since there are no precise internal or external dating points for the early part of the *Hellenica*. But G.E. Underhill argues convincingly that the comment on the expulsion of the Thirty and their adherents from Eleusis in 401/0, 'and even now they form a single state and the people keeps its oaths' (*Hell.* II.4.43), would have no real meaning if written more than ten or fifteen years after the event. This would suggest that Xenophon had the idea of continuing Thucydides, and began work on the project, at some time before about 390.

His *Hellenica* is a very considerable literary achievement. It is easy to read, lively and interesting. Xenophon was a popular writer in antiquity, counted as one of the first rate historians by Polybius, in the second century B.C., and Dionysius of Halicarnassus, in the first century B.C. Arrian, the historian of Alexander, modelled himself on Xenophon. Plutarch used Xenophon extensively as a source for his biographies, and in the second century A.D. Lucian of Samosata classed him with Herodotus and Thucydides. He was a perennial success with the reading public in antiquity and became recognised as a major author of the period of the definitive achievements of Attic literature.

All this is, necessarily, by way of contrast with the author of the *Hellenica Oxyrhynchia*. Whoever he was, he was certainly, by the canons of the classicism of the Hellenistic and Roman periods, a minor author. This does not necessarily mean that now he should be considered (insofar as his work is extant) a less good historian than Xenophon; but clearly he proved a less interesting writer from the point of view of the literary entertainment readers were looking for in the ancient world.

Commentators since the first edition have been remarking on the author's rather dry style, and restricted vocabulary. These can produce a monotonous effect from time to time, and are coupled with a feature of style, pretty clearly deliberate, which to the modern reader at least can seem tiresome. This is the use of digression. In the first two chapters of the London fragment there are three successive digressions from the main narrative - the first describing Athenian acts of hostility to Sparta before the sending of Demaenetus, the second commenting on Epicrates' and Cephalus' policy of opposition to Sparta (and wider anti-Spartanism) and the third dealing briefly with the case of Timolaus' change of sides to become an enemy of Sparta at Corinth. There are several other places in this comparatively short text where the technique of digression is the resource the author uses for interpreting or giving background to his narrative.

It needs to be stressed that this style of building up a narrative is capable of proving interesting. It depends very largely on what a reader expects or is used to. In the *Hellenica Oxyrhynchia* digressions are an analytical tool which has some flexibility. It is not known for certain whether the author made any use of speeches as analysis of events; only that there are none in the extant portions, unless a call to arms - nine words - is counted. But if a writer, even a continuator of Thucydides, felt the composition of appropriate speeches was a form of literary artifice which ought to be dropped in favour of an alternative, he could hardly be blamed for it.

Most of the characteristic techniques of the *Hellenica Oxyrhynchia* author are similarly capable, at least in theory, of being effective. But their repeated use, and the restricted range of style and vocabulary in the text, can be rather dull. Take for instance the style of sentence construction which involves beginning with the subject, using a participle with relative effect, then coming to the main clause. It occurs three times in Chapter 12 with not many sentences in between to give variety: "Agesilaus, staying there ... gave back the dead ...'; 'Tissaphernes, having learnt ... followed ...' and 'Agesilaus, going through the plain... led the army...'

But the effort made in the *Hellenica Oxyrhynchia* to produce a lively, or at least pleasing, narrative, goes quite deep. Throughout the text there is a low incidence of hiatus. This is particularly noticeable in the single brief bit of direct speech in the extant part of the text; a literal translation would be: '"let's go, O men" he said "of the city ..."' - and this brings out how the verb of speaking is delayed to an odd place because putting it in the normal slightly delayed position ('"let's go", he said "O men ..."') would create a hiatus. Other characteristic features are the use of parataxis (the particles *men* and *de*) - which is a very common feature in all Greek, but is still so prominent here that the reader is struck with how often it is used, and the use of litotes (e.g. I.1 'not with the agreement of the people'...).

Ephorus, the contemporary of Theopompus, used earlier writers' books to compose a history on a large scale, arranged by subjects rather than on a strict chronological framework. His books were widely read, and their popularity had something to do with the eventual supersession of earlier authors in the taste of the reading public. He began the tradition of compendious history whose doyen later on was Livy. Xenophon's works, and unsurprisingly those of Herodotus and Thucydides, survived this competition; and although his works were still there in Egypt in the early centuries A.D. the *Hellenica Oxyrhynchia* author did not survive to be copied in the medieval tradition. It is, at least in the literary entertainment dimension, a second rate work. The things which make it a precious text to the modern student are its provision of an alternative to Xenophon's story and certain parts of its analysis.

BIBLIOGRAPHY

This bibliography lists editions first and then other books and articles. Where a publication is referred to by an abbreviation in the Introduction or Commentary, this is given with the entry. All the books and articles listed have been used in preparing this book, but those not actually referred to in the Introduction or Commentary are marked with an asterisk (*).

1. Editions (in order of publication)

B.P. Grenfell and A.S. Hunt   'Theopompus (or Cratippus), Hellenica' in *Oxyrhynchus Papyri* V (London, 1908), pp.110−242.

─ ─ ─ ─ ─   Hellenica Oxyrhynchia cum Theopompi et Cratippi fragmentis (Oxford, 1909).

E. Meyer   *Theopomps Hellenika* (Halle, 1909).

J.H. Lipsius   *Cratippi Hellenicorum fragmenta Oxyrhynchia* (Kleine Texte für Vorlesungen und Übungen, 138, Bonn, 1916).

F. Jacoby   *Die Fragmente der griechischen Historiker* IIA pp.17−35 and IIC pp.6−20.

E. Kalinka   *Hellenika Oxyrhynchia* (Leipzig, 1927).

V. Bartoletti   'Nuovi frammenti delle "Elleniche di Ossirinco"' *Papiri greci e latini* 13.1 (1949), pp.61−81.

M. Gigante   *Le Elleniche di Ossirinco* (Rome, 1949).

P. Maas   'Nova Hellenicorum Oxyrhynchiorum Fragmenta' *CQ* 44 (1950), pp.8−11.

V. Bartoletti   *Hellenica Oxyrhynchia* (Leipzig, 1959).

L. Koenen   'Papyrology in the Federal Republic of Germany and Fieldwork of the International Photographic Archive in Cairo' *Studia Papyrologica* 15 (1976), pp.39−79 at pp.55−67 and 69−76.

G.A. Lehmann   'Ein neues fragment der Hell. Oxy.: einige Bemerkungen zu P. Cairo (temp. in v.no.) 26/6/27/1−35' *ZPE* 26 (1977), pp.181−191 at pp.189−190.

2. Other Books and Articles

S. Accame   'Trasibulo e i nuovi frammenti delle Elleniche di Ossirinco' *Riv. Fil.* n.s. 28 (1950), pp.30−49.

J.K. Anderson   'The Battle of Sardis in 395 B.C.' *CSCA* 7 (1974), pp.27−53.

A. Andrewes   'Lysias and the Theramenes Papyrus' *ZPE* 6 (1970), pp.35−38.
−−−−   'Notion and Cyzicus: the sources compared' *JHS* 102 (1982), pp.15−25.
G.L. Barber   *The Historian Ephorus* (London, 1935).
G. Barbieri   *Conone* (Rome, 1955).
K.J. Beloch   *Die Bevölkerung der griechisch − römischen welt* (Leipzig, 1886).
H. Bloch   'Studies in Historical Literature of the Fourth Century: I. The Hellenica of Oxyrhynchus and its authorship' *HSCP* supp.vol. I (1940), pp.303−341.
G. Bonamente   *Studio sulle Elleniche di Ossirinco* (Perugia, 1973).
R.J. Bonner   'The Boeotian Federal Constitution' *C.Phil.* 5 (1910), pp.405−417.
−−−−−   'The Four Senates of the Boeotians' *C.Phil.* 10 (1915), pp.381−385.
L.A. Botha   *The Hellenica Oxyrhynchia and the Asiatic Campaign of Agesilaus* (M.A. thesis, University of South Africa, 1980).
*H.R. Breitenbach   'Die Seeschlacht bei Notion (407−6)' *Hist.*20 (1971), pp.152−171.
I.A.F. Bruce   'Internal Politics and the Outbreak of the Corinthian War' *Emerita* 28 (1960), pp.75−86.
−−−−−   'Chios and P.S.I. 1304' *Phoenix* 18 (1964), pp.272−282.
−−−−−   *An Historical Commentary on the Hellenica Oxyrhynchia* (Cambridge, 1967) (= *Bruce*).
*J. Buckler   'The Re−establishment of the Boeotarchia (378 B.C.)' *AJAH* 4 (1979), pp.50−64.
G. Busolt   'Der neue Historiker und Xenophon' *Hermes* 43 (1908), pp.255−285.
*−−−−−   'Zur Glaubwürdigkeit Theopomps' *Hermes* 45 (1910), pp. 220−249.
*L. Canfora   *Tucidide Continuato* (Padua, 1970).
P. Cloché   'La politique thébaine de 404 à 396 av. J.−C.' *REG* 31 (1918), pp. 315−348.
−−−−−   *Thèbes de Béotie* (Namur, 1952).
*F. Cornelius   'Die Seeschlacht bei Sardes' *Klio* 26 (1933), pp. 29−31.
N.H. Demand   *Thebes in the Fifth Century B.C.* (London, 1982).
C. Dugas   'La Campagne d'Agésilas en Asie Mineure' *BCH* 34 (1910), pp. 58−95.
*C.J. Dull   'Thucydides I.113 and the leadership of Orchomenus' *C.Phil.* 72 (1977), pp.305−314.
*A. Fuks   'Note on the Nova Hellenicorum Oxyrhynchiorum

Fragmenta' *C.Q.* n.s.1 (1951), p.155.
G. Glotz 'Le conseil fédérale des Béotiens' *BCH* 32 (1908), pp.271−278.
A.W. Gomme 'Who was "Kratippos"?' *CQ* n.s.4 (1954), pp.53−55.
V.J. Gray 'Two different approaches to the battle of Sardis in 395 B.C.' *CSCA* 12 (1979), pp.183−200.
P. Harding 'The Theramenes Myth' *Phoenix* 28 (1974), pp. 101−111.
W.G. Hardy 'The Hellenica Oxyrhynchia and the Devastation of Attica' *C.Phil.* 21 (1926), pp.346−355.
B.V. Head *British Museum Coin Catalogue (Ionia)* (London, 1892).
A. Heinrichs 'Zur Interpretation des Michigan − Papyrus über Theramenes' *ZPE* 3 (1969), pp.101−108.
F. Jacoby *Die Fragmente der griechischen Historiker* (Berlin, 1923−) (= *FGrHist*).
*−−−−− 'The Authorship of the *Hellenica* of Oxyrhynchus' *CQ* 44 (1950), pp.1−11.
V. Kahrstedt *Forschungen zur Geschichte des ausgehenden fünften und des vierten Jahrhunderts* (Berlin, 1910).
J. Keil 'Zur Topographie und Geschichte von Ephesos' *JÖAI* 21−22 (1922−24), pp.96−112.
J. Kirchner *Prosopographia Attica* I−II (Berlin 1901 and 1903) (= Kirchner, *PA*).
L. Koenen 'Papyrology in the Federal Republic of Germany and Fieldwork of the International Photographic Archive in Cairo' *Studia Papyrologica* 15 (1976), pp.39−79.
J.A.O. Larsen 'The Boeotian Confederacy and Fifth−Century Oligarchic Theory' *TAPA* 86 (1955), pp.40−50.
−−−−− *Representative Government in Greek and Roman History* (Berkeley and Los Angeles, 1955).
G.A. Lehmann 'Ein Historiker namens Kratippos' *ZPE* 23 (1976), pp.265−288.
*−−−−− 'Ein neues Fragment der Hell. Oxy.: einige Bemerkungen zu P. Cairo (temp.inv.no.) 26/6/27/1−35' *ZPE* 26 (1977), pp.181−191.
−−−−− 'Spartas Arche und die Vorphase des Korinthischen Krieges in den Hellenica Oxyrhynchia' I: *ZPE* 28 (1978), pp.109−128; II: *ZPE* 30 (1978), pp.73−93.
D.M. Lewis *Sparta and Persia* (Leiden, 1977).
E.C. Marchant and G.E. Underhill *Xenophon: Hellenica* (Oxford, 1906).
R. Merkelbach and H.C. Youtie 'Ein Michigan−Papyrus über Theramenes' *ZPE* 2 (1968), pp.161−169.

*D. Nellen   'Zur Darstellung der Schlacht bei Sardes in der Quellen' *Anc.Soc.* 3 (1972), pp.45−54.

P. Pédech   'Un historien nommé Cratippe, *REA* 92 (1970), pp.31−45.

C. Préaux   rev. of V. Bartoletti 'Nuovi frammenti delle Elleniche di Ossirinco' *Chronique d'Égypte* 48 (1949), pp.348−350.

*W.K. Prentice   'Thucydides and Cratippus' *C.Phil.* 22 (1977), pp.399−408.

W.K. Pritchett   *The Greek State at War*, I, II and III (Berkeley and Los Angeles, 1974−) (= *Pritchett* I, II, III).

*W. Rhys Roberts   'Theopompus in the Greek Literary Critics' *CR* 22 (1908), pp.118−122.

E. Ruschenbusch   'Theopompea: antipoliteuesthai' *ZPE* 39 (1980), pp.81−90.

*G. de Sanctis   'La battaglia di Notion' *Riv.Fil.* 59 (1931), pp.222−239.

H. Swoboda   'Studien zur Verfassung Boeotiens' *Klio* 10 (1910), pp.315−334.

R.J.A. Talbert   *Atlas of Classical History* (London and Sydney, 1985).

M. Treu   'Einwände gegen die Demokratie in der Literatur des 5./4. Jh.' *Studii Clasice* 12 (1970), pp.17−31.

G.E. Underhill   see E.C. Marchant.

−−−−−   'Theopompus (or Cratippus), Hellenica' *JHS* 28 (1908), pp.277−90.

J. Wackernagel   'Orthographica und Verwandtes' *Philologus* 86 (1930), pp.133−144.

H. Wankel   'Sprachliche Bemerkungen zu dem neuen Fragment der Hellenika Oxyrhynchia' *ZPE* 29 (1978), pp.54−56.

H.D. Westlake   'Rival Traditions on a Rhodian Stasis' *MH* 40 (1983), pp.239−250.

*U. Wilcken   'Ein Theopompfragment in der neuen Hellenika' *Hermes* 43 (1908), pp.475−477.

H.C. Youtie   see R. Merkelbach.

CAIRO.
FRAGMENTS

Col. I

FR.1
1 [.].ς προσβαλεῖν τοῖς τε[ίχεσι .... τὰς]
   [π]λείστας τῶν τριήρω[ν .... τὰς]
   [δ'] ἑτέρας τόπον τῆς Ἐφε[σίας..... .....]
   [ἐκ]βι[βά]σας δὲ πᾶσαν τὴν [δύναμιν..... .]
5 [..]ω ἐπὶ τῆς πόλεως. Ἐφέσιοι [δὲ ... τῶν Λα—]
   [κε]δαιμονίων αὐτοῖς .... [..... . τοὺς]
   [μὲ]ν μετὰ τοῦ Πασίωνος τῶν Ἀθηναίων
   [οὐχ] ἑώρων — ἔτυχον γὰρ ὄντες ἔτι πορρω καὶ
   [μα]κροτέραν ὁδὸν τῶν ἑτέρων βαδιζοντες —
10 [τοὺ]ς δὲ περὶ τὸν Θράσυλλον ὁρῶντ[ε]ς ὅσον
   [οὔ]πω παρόντας ἀπήντων αὐτοῖς πρὸς
   [τὸ]ν λιμένα τὸν Κορησσὸν καλούμενον
   [ἔχο]ντες συμμάχους τούς τε βοηθήσαντας
   [....]..π[.]...[.]ον καὶ πιστοτάτο[υ]ς .ο.ε..
15 [....].... νητωνηκ[.].τ.....[.]ε[.]...[]
   [...]βι[.]. πεδίωι κατοικούντων. μ[ετ]ὰ δὲ
   [ταῦ]τα Θράσυλλος μὲν ὁ τῶν Ἀθηναίων
   [στρα]τηγός, ὡς ἧκε πρὸς τὴν πόλι[ν, ἔλι]πέν
   [τιν]ας μὲν τῶν στρατιωτῶν προσβα-
20 [λό]ντας, τοὺς δὲ πρὸς τὸν λόφον α[.]...
   [...]σηγεν ὅς ὑψηλὸς καὶ δύσβατός ἐστιν. ...
   [..μ]ὲν ἐκτὸς ἔστραπται, τὰ δ'ἔξω τῆς πό—
   [λεως]. τῶν δ' Ἐφεσίων ἡγοῦντο καὶ Τίμαρ—
   [χο]ς καὶ Ποσσικράτης οἱ][
25 [..... .]..βει[
   [
   [
   [
   [

FR.2[
   [..... ....]σ[.].[
   [..... ....]υτους. πρα.[
   [..... ....]σι τινας τῶν[
   [..... ....]μα νουντ[
35 [..... ....]ντας. .α[

Cairo Fragments — Translation

... to attack the walls ...
... most of the triremes ...
... the others, a place in Ephesian territory ...
... having disembarked the whole force ... on the city.
[But] the Ephesians with the Spartans ... them ...
... they did not see those of the Athenians with Pasion (since they were still a long way away and marching by a longer route than the others), but seeing those with Thrasyllus, who had only just arrived, they met them in battle at the harbour called Coressus, having as allies those who had helped [them previously] and the most reliable ...

...living [in the Kil]bi[an] plain. After this Thrasyllus, the general of the Athenians, as he reached the city, left some of his soldiers attacking, but led others to the hill, which is high and hard to climb. [In this way] some were turned to retreat inside, and some outside, the city. The leaders of the Ephesians were Timarchus and Possicrates ...

FR.1 +3

Col. II

γης.[
πιλ[..]..αλ[
μιβ.. Θρασ[υλλ
τας [.]..ειπ[
40 ται. ἐπειδὴ δὲ προ[
.[..] πρὸς καρτερὰ χωρ[ί]α [
.[..]. καὶ πρὸς αὐτοὺς κατέφευ[γον .... τὸ]
στρατ[ό]πεδον ἐπῆγεν. ὑποχ[ω]ρούντων
δὲ τῶν ἐναντίων οἱ μὲν Ἀθηναῖοι προ-
45 θύμως ἐπηκολούθουν ὡς κ[α]τὰ κράτος
ληψ[ό]μενοι τὴν πόλιν. Τίμαρχος δ[ὲ] καὶ
Πο[σσ]ικράτης οἱ τῶν Ἐφεσίων ἡγε[μόν]ες
ἀνεκαλοῦντο τοὺς ἑαυτῶν ὁπλίτας[. παρ]ελ-
θόντων δὲ τῶν Ἀθηναίων ..[..... ...]ν-
50 τες πάλιν ο[ἱ] ψιλοὶ τῶν ἀνοδ[εύτων ...]
εἰσβάλλουσι μετὰ τῶν .ο..τ.[..... .]η
[....]. οἱ δὲ διὰ τὴν τῶ[ν .... μ]ε-
τὰ δ[ὲ β]ραχὺν χρόνον .[
ρο[.]ν. ἐπέπεσεν τῶ[ι
55 ἀπ[οπει]ρώμεν[ο]ι[κατα-]
πλαγέντες διέλυσα[ν].[
πρὸς τὰς ναῦς ἀτάκτως [
ἔφευγον. ὅσοι μὲν οὖν αὐτῶν τ[ὴν εἰς θά-]
λατταν ὁδὸν ἀπεχώρουν, ἀσφα[λῶς ἐπο-]
60 [ρεύ]θησαν. τῶν δὲ τὴν ἄνωθε[ν ὁδὸν ἐλθόν-]
[των..... . διε]φθάρησαν ..[
[..... .....]ωσεν δι' αὐτοῦ[
[..... .....]ον ... πεμφα.[
[..... .....]ων κατ[.].[
[..... .....]πρε..με.[

---

50 ἀν ὁδ[ῶν Wankel.

... to strong places ...
... and fled to them ...
... he led the army forward. Since the enemy were retreating, the Athenians followed them eagerly with the intention of taking the city by force. But Timarchus and Possicrates, the leaders of the Ephesians, called up their own hoplites. When the Athenians approached ...
... the light—armed soldiers going back from trackless ... made an assault with the ...
... but they, because of the ... of the ...
... but after a short time ...

... being surprised they fell apart ...
... towards the ships in disorder ...
... they fled. As many of them as retreated by the road to the sea, marched safely. But of those going by the upper road ... were destroyed ...

Col. III

[.....] ..... .[
[.....].[.].ς οι προ[
[.....]ον ἀποβ....[
[στρα]τιωτῶν παρ[
70 [...]ως ὑπὸ το[ῦ] πράτ[τ..... ..... .εἰς
[Συρ]ακούσας [...] δι[
[..τ]ῆς σαφηνε[ί]ας] .[
π[.].εων..αιν.[
ἵπ[π]αρχον[.]....[
75 ἐκεῖνος ...[.]..[
τοῖς στρατιώτα[ι]ς [
τῆς Ἐφέσου .[
ἐπιμείναντες α[..... ....κιν−]
δυνεύειν [.]π.[
80 χώρισε καὶ[
τα..... .[
[..]ονε[

**FLORENCE
FRAGMENTS**

A

I -] . αιχα[. | . . . .]ντων
[. . | . . . .] . [. .] τετρακ[ο |⁵ σι . . . .
. . . .]ν προτρο[πάδ]η ἐ|[τράπησαν, οἱ δὲ] Λα-
κεδαιμό[νιοι .]ωρι . ! [. . . . .]. ὐ[π]εχώρου[ν ἐν]
τάξει | [πρὸς τοὺς λόφο]υς. οἱ δὲ στρατιῶ[τα]ι τῶν | [Ἀθη-
ναίων το]ὐτους μὲν οὐκ ἐδίωξαν, | ¹⁰[τοῖς δὲ Μεγαρε]ῦσι⟨ν⟩
[ἐ]πακολουθοῦντες ἐ|[πὶ . . . .] ὁδοῦ τῆς πρὸς τὴν
π[όλιν φερούσης] καταβάλλουσιν αὐτῶν [ἀριθμὸν πολύ]ν.
μετὰ δὲ ταῦτα καταδρα[μόντες τὴν χ]ώραν καὶ τοὺς νεκροὺς |
¹⁵[ἀποδόντες ὑπο]σπόνδους τῶν Μεγαρέ[ων] κα[ὶ τοὺς   10
τῶ]ν Λακεδ[α]ιμονίων (ἀπέ[θα]ρον [δὲ το]ύτων ὡς εἴκοσιν)
ἱστᾶσιν [τρ]οπαῖ[ον · τ]αῦτα δὲ ποιήσαντες ἀνεχώ[ρ]ησαν
πάλιν ἐπ' οἴκου. 2 Ἀθηναῖοι δὲ πυ|²⁰[θ]όμενοι τὰ περὶ τῆς
μάχης τοῖς μὲν [στ]ρατηγοῖς ὠργίζοντο καὶ χαλεπῶς
εἶ[χο]ν ὑπολαμβάνοντες [π]ροπετῶς αὐ[το]ὺς ἀνελέσθαι
τὸν κίνδ[υ]νον καὶ κυ[βε]ῦσαι περὶ ὅλης τῆς πόλεως, ἐπὶ
δὲ τῇ | ²⁵[νί]κῃ περι[χα]ρεῖ[ς] ἦσαν· ἐ[τ]ύγχανον γὰρ
[Λα]κεδαιμον[ίω]ν οὐδέποτε πρότερον κ[ε|κρατη]κότες
[. . . . . .] περὶ Π[ύλο]ν . . [.]α|[. . . . .] . . . . [. . . . .
. . . .]αν|[-   20

---

3   ἐ[τραπησαν   Bartoletti, *exempli gratia*.
5   λόφου]ς   Castiglioni.
8   φερούσης]...[ἀριθμὸν πολύ]ν   Maas,
    exempli gratia.
10 τῶν Μεγαρέ[ων ἑ]κα[τόν, τῶ]ν
    Λακεδαιμονίων ἀπο[θα]νόν[των α]ὐτῶν
    ὡς κτλ.   Bartoletti in ed. I. As
    Bartoletti comments, there is too little
    room on the papyrus for [ων ἑ].

36

Florence Fragments — Translation

I.1 ... four hundred ... they were driven headlong, but the Spartans ... retreated in order to the hills. But the soldiers of the Athenians did not pursue these men, but followed the Megarians ... on the road ... leading to the city they struck down a great number of them. After this, having ravaged the land and having given back, under a truce, the dead of the Megarians and of the Spartans (about twenty of these died), they set up a trophy. Having done these things they withdrew back home.

I.2 But the Athenians, having found out about the battle, were angry with the generals and took a hostile attitude, supposing that they had undertaken the risk rashly and played dice with the whole of the city at stake. But they were glad at the victory, for as it happened they had never before beaten the Spartans [since the affair] at Pylos ...

desunt versus nonnulli

II -]τ[. . . . .] . . [- - -]|ν[. . . .]τ . [.]ϱ . [- - -]|η . [.. . .]στρατε[- - -]|π . [. χ]ϱήματα [- - -]|⁵σαν [ἀ]ναγ-καζ[- - -]|τυχ[.]ν ἰδιωτ[- - -] | οὐδ[ὲ]ν ἧττον [- - -] | τω[. . . .]ις εἰῶ[- - -]|. .[. .]ϱ[.]ων κα[- - -] | ¹⁰ἐξ [αὐτ]ῆς τῆς [- - -] | γε[. . . . .]επ[- - -] | ωσ . [- - -] | των [- - -] | χου[.]ιω . [- - -]|¹⁵ται προσ[- - -]|χρω[- - -] | . . [- - - ἐπι]|τηδευμ[- - -] | μηνα.[.]ψ[- - -] | ²⁰τος καταπο[- - -]| ϱος αὐτίκα [- - -]|τα κατὰ τὴν [- - -]|οις ὁ Πεδάρι[τος - - -] | ἀρχὴν ἐπηγα[γ - - -] | ²⁵οὔθ' οἵτινες ἐ.[- - - δυ-]|ναστείαν, οὐδ[- - - φι]|λοτιμίας ἀπε.[- - -]|νως διέσω- 30 σαν τη[- - -] | Ἀθηναίων ητ[- - -] | ³⁰ατη γενομένη [- - - πε]|ρὶ ἧς καὶ Θουκ[υδίδης - - -] | Πε{ρι}δαριτο[- - -] | μεν τῶν α[- - -]|τες εὐθέως [- - -] | ³⁵τατην να[- - -] | [. . . . . .]κ[-

B

III -]ην | [- - -] μεθ' ἡμέ|[ραν - - -] . . ατησε|[- - -] . . . . αι | ⁵[- - -] . ν ἡμέραν | [- - -]των τὸν | [- - -]ιρας καλου|[μεν - - -]ιτο μὲν | [- - -]ων δὲ προσ | ¹⁰[- - -] ξανεν | [- - -]εκλε | [- - -]πλευ | [- - -]ουθ . . . | [- - -] νησι | ¹⁵[- - -]ουσας | [- - -]ι ἐρῆμοι | [- - - ἀ]φελομε|[ν - - -] βασιλέ|[ως - - -]ασεπο | ²⁰[- - -]ς νήσοις |[- - -]ς 40 εκει|[- - -] ταῖς Κλα|[ζομεναῖς - - -] . ησος | [- - -] . . [.]τρ | ²⁵[- - -] | [- - -]σον | [- - -]ς ἄριστα |[- - -] . . τον | [- - -]ντω ταυ |³⁰[- - -] μὴ προσ|[- - -]θειρ . | [-

---
32 περὶ <Πε>δαριτο[Bartoletti in ed.I.

desunt versus saltem III

IV _]νησιῷ[. ὥ]σπερ ἐξιώ[θει . . . .]|ρας ἐκπ[έ]μπειν ν[αῦς . . . .] | αὐτάς, πληρώσας τρ[ιήρεις δέκα τὰς ἄριστα] | ⁵πλεούσας, τὰς μὲν ἑτ[έρας ἐκέλευσε ναυ]λοχεῖν ἕως ἂν ἀπάρω[σιν αἱ τῶν πολεμί]ων πόρρω τῆς γῆς, [αὐτὸς δὲ τ . . . . προ]έπλει πρὸς τὴν Ἔφεσ[ον . . . .] προσαξόμενος αὐτά[ς. **2** Λύσανδρος δὲ κατι]|¹⁰δὼν α[ὐ]τοὺς τρεῖς να[ῦς εὐθὺς 50 καθεῖλκεν· αἵ]|περ κα[ὶ] πρότερον αὐ[τ . . . .]| καταδύ[ο]υσι τὸν Ἀ[ν]τ[ίοχον . . . .]|ως καὶ διαφθείρου[σιν . . . . τῶν] μὲν Ἀθηναίων φ[οβηθέντες οἱ συμπλέον]|¹⁵τες εὐθέως πρὸς τἄ[μπαλιν ἐτράπησαν οὐ] προνοούμενοι τ[ὸ να]υμα[χῆσαι κατὰ κρά]τος Λύσανδρος δὲ ἀ[ν]αλαβ[ὼν πάσας τὰς τρι]ήρεις ἐδίωκε τοὺς [π]ολεμ[ίους. **3** οἱ δὲ λοιποὶ] τῶν Ἀθηναίων κ[α]τιδόν[τες ἀπηρκότας] | ²⁰τοὺς Λακεδαιμον[ίου]ς καὶ δ[ιώκοντας τὴν] αὐτῶν δεκαναῖα[ν] ἐνέβ[ησαν μὲν εὐθέως,] ἐπειγόμενοι βοηθῆσαι τα[ῖς αὐτῶν ναυσίν·] ἐπικειμένων δὲ τῶν ἐν- 60 [αντίων ἤδη διὰ] ταχέων πάσας μὲν οὐκ ἠ[δύναντο τὰς] | ²⁵τριήρεις φθῆναι π[λ]ηρώ[σαντες, ταῖς δὲ] πλείσταις αὐτῶν μ[ι]κρὸν [ἐκ τοῦ λιμέ]νος ἀναχθέντες το[ῦ τ]ῶν [Κολοφωνίων] τὰς μὲν προπλευ[σά]σας [. . . . . ,] αὐτοὶ δὲ ταραχθέντες ἀμα[χεὶ . . . .] | ³⁰καὶ δι'

44 νησι δ Maas: the very sharply angled bottom left corner of a letter is preserved: Πελοπον]νησιῳ̣[ν ? Bartoletti.
50 καὶ δέκα M.H. Crawford.
54 τὰ[ς ἀφορμὰς ἔφευγον Bartoletti in ed. I.
57 κατιδόν[τες κρατοῦντας ἤδη] Maas.
60 τα[ῖς προπλευσάσαις Maas, τα[ῖς διωκομέναις Wade–Gery in a letter to Bartoletti.
65 ἅμα [ἐναυμάχησαν Bartoletti in ed. I.

IV.1 ... as was customary ... to send ships ... them, having manned the ten swiftest−sailing triremes, he ordered the others to lie in wait until those of the enemy should have moved far off from the land, but he himself sailed ahead to Ephesus ... about to bring them over to himself.

IV.2 But Lysander, when he saw them, immediately launched thirteen ships; which also formerly ... they sank Antiochus ... and they destroyed ... those of the Athenians who were sailing together turned back in fright and fled, since they did not intend to give battle in force: but Lysander took all his triremes and pursued the enemy.

IV.3 But the remaining Athenians, seeing that the Spartans had sailed away and were pursuing their force of ten ships, embarked quickly, hurrying to come to the aid of their own ships. But as the enemies were already approaching quickly they could not get the triremes manned before they arrived; but having advanced a little way from the harbour of the Colophonians with most of them, the ones sailing in the vanguard ... but they in confusion without fighting ... and they retreated from

ἀταξίαν ὑπεχώρη[σαν τοῖς πολε]μίοις. Λακεδαιμόνιοι
δὲ κα[τιδόντες φεύ]γον[τα]ς τοὺς Ἀθηνα[ί]ους ἐπε[νεχθέν-
τες δι]αφθείρουσιν αὐτῶν καὶ λα[μβάνουσιν εἴ]κοσι καὶ δύο
ναῦς, τὰς δὲ λοιπὰ[ς εἰς τὸ Νότι | ³⁵ο]ν κατέκλεισαν.
4 ἐκεῖνοι μὲν ο[ὖν διαπραξά]μενοι ταῦτα καὶ τροπαῖον 70
στ[ήσαντες] πρὸς τῷ λιμένι τῆς πόλεως εἰς [τἄμπα]λιν
ἀπῆλθον· Ἀθηναῖοι δὲ παραν[τίκα μὲν] ἡ[σ]υχίαν εἶχον,
παρελθουσῶ[ν δὲ . . . . . .] | ⁴⁰τριῶν ἡμερῶν θεραπεύ-
σ[αντες . . . . . ||

C

V _]α̣[..]αὐτ̣[. . . . .] | [. . . .]. . . . . . . εἰώ-
θει γὰ[ρ . . . . ὁ]μολογίας εὐθέως .[. . . . . . .
τοὺς | φυγ]άδας. 2 παρ' αὐτῷ μὲν γ[ὰρ . . . .]ν ἐ̣ν | ⁵[τῷ
νε]ῷ̣ τῷ τῆς Δήμητρ[ος καὶ Κό]ρης, δ̣[ς | . . . .]γε τοῖς
τείχεσί ἐστι [. . . . .]ου διὰ τὴν [. . . .]ν ἐγεγόνει τῇ [ὕλῃ,
νύκ]τ̣ωρ̣ [δ]ὲ κατα[στὰς] τὸν μὲν ⟨ἄλλον⟩ χρόνον [ἡσυ]χίαν 80
εἶχεν [ἐγκρ]ύψας αὐτὸν εἰς τὴ[ν] ὕλην· ὅτε δὲ | ¹⁰[κατα-
σ]ταίη φύλαξ ὁ Ἀθη[ναῖο]ς, ἐκεῖνος μὲν καθεὶς ὑπὲρ τοῦ
τείχ[ους] σπάρτον ἐποίησεν [ἄ]ν τι σημεῖον ὅτ[ι] παρε[ί-]
ληφεν τὴ[ν φ]υλακήν, ἢ φθεγξάμενο[ς ἢ λί]θῳ βαλών, ὁ
δὲ Μύνδ⟨ι⟩ος ἐξελ[θὼν ἐ]κ τῆς | ¹⁵ὕλης πρῶτον μὲν εἴ τι
γραμματεῖον εἴη παρ' ἐκείνου καθειμένον [τε] ἐλάμβα-
[νε]ν καὶ διεφύλαττ[ε]ν, [ἔπειτ]α δὲ προ[σ]ῆψεν αὐτὸς ἂν
ἕτερον [τῷ σπάρτῳ γ]ραμμ[α||τεῖον

---

79 [τῆς Χί]ου   Bartoletti suggests.
80 ⟨ἄλλον⟩   Bartoletti.
85 Μυνδ⟨ι⟩ος   Maas, Μύνδος De
    Sanctis in a letter to Bartoletti, μυνδὸς
    Bartoletti in ed. I.
87 ἐλάμβαν' ἄν   M.H. Crawford.
88 [τῷ ἑτέρῳ γ] κτλ.   Vogliano.

the enemy in confusion. But the Spartans seeing the Athenians fleeing pressed on and destroyed or captured twenty—two ships, and blockaded the rest in Notium.

IV.4 So they, having carried out these things, set up a trophy by the harbour of the city and turned back. The Athenians for the time being kept quiet, but when ... went past ... for three days having looked after ...

V.1 ... the exiles ...

V.2 For with him ... in the temple of Demeter and Persephone, which is [near?] the walls ... through the ... had happened ... the wood ... but he stood about at night and kept quiet for some time having hidden himself in the wood. But when the Athenian was standing at his post he, letting down a rope over the wall, would make a sign that he had taken over the guard duty, either by calling or by throwing a stone, and the Myndian coming out of the wood first of all would take and keep any note that might have been let down by him; then he would himself attach another note to the rope.

desunt versus nonnulli

3 -]| ν̣ [- - -]|ι̣οντ̣α[- - -]|| τὸ τεῖχ[ος - - -]|χου εξ[-
- -]|⁵νν . [- - -] | φυλ̣[α - - -]|·ε̣[· ·]ο̣ · [- - -] | τ̣ων οιγ[- 90
- -]|ε̣πλη.[- - -]|¹⁰τερα[- - -]|ϑεν α̣[- - -]|[·]· ·[-

D

    - - - -   ⁵ ὀλ]ίγῳ πλεί[ους
  ]εχοντ[τ]οῖς ἱπ[πεῦσι
  ]ωνου[   ]δυο.[
τετ]αγμέν[- - - -
  ].στησ.[

---

92 The papyrus shows ΙΓΟΪΠΛΕΙ — the omega written above, apparently as a correction.

LONDON
FRAGMENTS

A

VI (I) Ὑπὸ δὲ τοὺ[ς αὐτοὺς χρόνο]υς ἐξέπλευσε τριήρης | Ἀθήνηθεν [οὐ μετὰ τῆς τοῦ] δήμου γνώμης, ἧ[ν] | δὲ Δημαίν[ετ]ος ὁ κύ[ρ]ιος αὐτῆς κοινωσάμενο[ς ἐν] | ἀπορ⟨ρ⟩ήτῳ τ[ῇ β]ουλῇ, ὡς λέγεται, περὶ τοῦ πράγ-[ματος] | ⁵ἐπειδὴ [σ]υν[έσ]τησαν αὐτῷ τ[ῶν] πολιτῶν· σὺν [οἷς] | καταβὰς εἰς Πειραιᾶ καὶ καθ[ελκύσας] ναῦν ἐκ τ[ῶ]ν νεωσοίκων ἀναγόμεν[ος ἔ]πλει πρὸ]ς Κόν[ων]α. **2** θορύβου δὲ μετὰ ταῦτα γε[νομένου,] καὶ τ[ῶν] Ἀθηναίων ἀγανακτούντω[ν ὅσοι γνώ]ριμ[οι κ]αὶ χα|¹⁰ρίεντες ἦσαν καὶ λεγ[όντων ὅτι κατα]βα[λοῦ]σι τὴν πόλιν ἄρχοντες 10 πολέ[μου πρὸς Λακ]εδαιμον[ί]ους, καταπλαγέντες οἱ β[ουλευταὶ τὸ]ν θόρυβον συνήγαγον τὸν δῆμον οὐθὲν προσ[π]οιούμενοι μετεσχηκέναι τοῦ πράγματος. συνεληλυθότος δὲ | ¹⁵τοῦ πλήθους ἀνιστάμενοι τῶν Ἀθηναίων οἵ τε περὶ Θρασύβουλον καὶ Αἴσιμον καὶ Ἄνυτον ἐδίδασκον αὐτοὺς ὅτι μέγαν ⟨ἂν⟩αιροῦνται κίνδυνον εἰ μὴ τὴν πόλιν ἀπολύσουσι τῆς αἰτίας. **3** τῶν δὲ Ἀθηναίων οἱ μὲν ἐπ⟨ι⟩εικεῖς καὶ τὰς οὐσίας ἔχοντες ἔ|²⁰στεργον τὰ παρόντα, οἱ δὲ πολλοὶ καὶ δημοτικοὶ τότε μὲν φοβηθέντες ἐπείσθησαν τοῖς συμβουλεύουσι, καὶ πέμψαντες πρὸς Μίλωνα τὸν 20 ἁρμοστὴν τὸν Αἰγίνης εἶπο[ν] ὅπως δύ[ν]αται τιμωρεῖσθαι τὸν Δημαί[νε]τον, ὡς ο[ὐ με]τὰ τῆς πόλεως ταῦτα | ²⁵πεποιηκότα· [ἔμ]προσθ[εν δὲ σ]χεδὸν ἅπαντα τὸν χρόνον ἐτάρ[ατ]τον τ[ὰ πράγ]ματα καὶ πολλὰ τ[ο]ῖς Λακεδαιμο-

---

10 κατα]βα[λοῦ]σι Rühl; δια]βα[λοῦ]σι
    Grenfell and Hunt.
16 papyrus reads αἱροῦνται:
    ⟨ἀν⟩αιροῦνται Richards: cf. I.2
    above.

London Fragments — Translation

VI.1 About the same time a trireme sailed out from Athens without the agreement of the people. In charge of it was Demaenetus who had, it is said, made a secret agreement with the Council concerning this affair, since some of the citizens supported him. With them he went down to Piraeus, launched a ship from the shipsheds, and, putting to sea, was on his way to Conon.

VI.2 Thereupon there was a great outcry. Those of the Athenians who were well-born and cultivated were indignant, saying that they would destroy the city by beginning a war with the Spartans. The Councillors were alarmed by the outcry and called the people together, making out that they had had no share in the affair. When the people were assembled, the party of the Athenians supporting Thrasybulus, Aesimus and Anytus got up and instructed them that they risked great danger unless they absolved the city from responsibility.

VI.3 Those of the Athenians who were moderates and men of property were happy with the existing situation; but the majority of the populace, although they were then in a state of fear and, persuaded by those who advised them, sent envoys to Milon, the harmost of Aegina, to tell him how he could punish Demaenetus who had not acted with the city's approval, had previously almost the whole time stirred up matters and acted much in opposition to the Spartans.

[νίοι]ς ἀ[ντέπρα]ττον. **VII (II)** ἀπέπεμπ[ο]ν μὲν γὰρ ὅπλ[α τε καὶ ὑπη]ρεσίας ἐπὶ τὰς ναῦς τὰς μετὰ τοῦ Κ[όνωνος, ἐπέμ]φθησαν δὲ πρέσβ[ει]ς | ³⁰ὡς βασιλέα π[.... οἱ περὶ ..].. κράτη τε καὶ Ἁγνίαν καὶ Τελε[σήγ]ορον· οὓς καὶ συλλοβὼν Φάραξ ὁ πρότερον ναύαρχος ἀπέστειλε πρὸς τοὺς Λ[α]κεδαιμονίους, οἱ δ᾽ [ἀ]πέκτειναν αὐτούς. 30 **2** ἠναντιοῦντο δὲ ταῦτα παροξυνόντων τῶν περὶ τὸν | ³⁵Ἐπικράτη καὶ Κέφαλον· οὗτοι γὰρ ἔτυχον ἐπιθυμοῦντες ⟨ἐκπολεμῶσαι⟩ μάλιστα τὴν πόλιν, καὶ ταύτην ἔσχον ⟨τὴν γνώμην⟩ οὐκ ἐπειδὴ Τιμοκράτει διελέχθησαν καὶ [τ]ὸ || χρυσίον [ἔλαβον, ἀλλ᾽ ἤδη πολὺ] πρότερον. καίτοι τινὲς λέγ[ουσιν αἴτια γενέσθ]αι τὰ παρ᾽ ἐκείνου χρήματα τ[οῦ σ]ṭ[στῆναι τούτους καὶ] τοὺς ἐν Βοιωτοῖς καὶ τοὺς ẹ[ν τ]ạ[ῖς ἄλλαις πόλεσι τ]αῖς προειρημένα[ις,] | ⁵οὐκ εἰδότες ὅτι π[ᾶσιν αὐτοῖς συ]νεβεβήκει πάλαι δυσμενῶς ἔχειν [πρὸς Λακεδαιμο]νί[ο]υς καὶ σκοπεῖν ὅπως ἐκπολεμώ- 40 [σουσι] τ[ὰς πόλει]ς. ἐμίσουν γὰρ οἱ μὲν Ἀργεῖοι καὶ Βọιωτ[οὶ ....]ṛωται τοὺς Λακεδαιμονίους ὅτι τοῖς ἐναν-[τίοι]ς τῶν πολιτῶν | ¹⁰αὐτοῖς ἐχρῶντο φίλοις, [ο]ἱ δ᾽ [ἐ]ν

---

25 papyrus shows]ττεν, but the ε seems
to have been corrected to an ο.
27 ἐπέμ]φθησαν: only the upper part of the
down-stroke of the φ is visible;
ἐπορε]ύθησαν Boissevain.
π[...could also be γ[...
28 papyrus shows]τοκρατη or]π[.]κρατη
Αὐ]τοκράτη or Ἱπ]ποκράτη Grenfell
and Hunt.
33 ταύτην ἔσχον ⟨τὴν γνώμην⟩ Fuhr;
ταύτην ⟨τὴν γνώμην⟩ ἔσχον
Grenfell and Hunt.
35 ἀλλ᾽ ἤδη Wilcken; ἀλλα καὶ Grenfell
and Hunt.
42 Βοιωτ[ῶν προσ]τ⟨ά⟩ται Castiglioni.

VII.1 For they were in the habit of sending weapons and crews to the ships under Conon, and those with ... crates and Hagnias and Telesegorus had been sent as envoys to the King. Pharax, the former nauarch, arrested them and sent them to the Spartans who put them to death.

VII.2 They took this position of opposition to Sparta under the encouragement of those supporting Epicrates and Cephalus, for these men were keen to involve the city in war, and had this intention not when they had dealings with Timocrates and took the gold but already a long time before that. And yet some say that the money from him was the cause of concerted action by these people and some of the Boeotians and some in the other cities previously mentioned. But they do not know that all had long been ill—disposed towards the Spartans, looking out for a way that they might make the cities adopt a war policy. For the Argives and the Boeotians hated the Spartans because they treated as friends their enemies among the citizens; and those who

ταῖς Ἀθήναις ἐπιθυμοῦντες ἀπαλλάξαι τ[οὺ]ς Ἀθηνα[ί]ους
τῆς ἡσυχίας καὶ τῆς εἰρήνης καὶ [πρ]οαγαγεῖν ἐπὶ τὸ
πολεμεῖν καὶ π[ολ]υπρα[γ]μονεῖν, ἵν' αὐτοῖς ἐκ τῶν κοινῶν
ᾖ χρηματίζεσ[θ]αι. 3 τῶν δὲ Κορινθίων | [15] οἱ μεταστῆσαι
τὰ πρά[γμ]ατα ζητοῦντες οἱ μὲν ἄλλοι ⟨παραπλησίως⟩ τοῖς
Ἀργείοις καὶ τοῖς Βοιωτοῖς ἔτυχον δυσμ[ε]νῶς διακείμενοι
πρὸς τοὺς Λακεδαιμονίους, Τ[ιμό]λαος δὲ μόνος αὐτοῖς διά- 50
φορος γεγονὼς ἰδ[ί]ων ἐγκλημάτων ἕνεκα, πρότερον ἄριστα
διακεί'μεν[ος] | [20] καὶ μάλιστα λακωνίζων, ὡς ἔξεστι κατα-
μαθεῖν ἐκ τῶν κατὰ τὸν πόλεμον συ[μ]βάντων τὸν Δεκ[ε-]
λεικόν. 4 ἐκεῖνος γὰρ ὁτὲ μὲν πενταναΐαν ἔχων ἐπόρθησε
τῶν νήσων τινὰς τῶν ἐπ' Ἀθηναίο[ι]ς οὐσῶν, ὁτὲ δὲ μετὰ
δύο τ[ρ]ιήρων εἰς Ἀμφίπολιν | [25] καταπλεύσας καὶ παρ'
ἐ[κεί]νων ἑτέρας τέτ[τα]ρας συμπληρωσάμ[ενος ἐνίκη]σε
Σί⟨μιχ⟩ον ναυμ[αχ]ῶν τὸν στρατηγὸν [τῶν Ἀθηνα]ίων,
ὥσπερ εἴρηκ[ά π]ου καὶ πρότερον, κ[αὶ τριήρε]ις τὰς
πολεμ[ί]ας [ἔλα]βεν οὔσας πέντε κ[αὶ ναῦς ἃς ἔπ]εμψαν 60
τριά[κοντ]α · | [30] μετὰ δὲ ταῦτα [........] ἔχων τρι-
ήρ[εις] καταπλεύσας εἰς Θάσ[ο]ν ἀπέστησε ταύτην τ[ῶ]ν
Ἀθηναίων. 5 οἱ μὲν οὖν ἐν ταῖς πόλεσι ταῖς προειρημέναις
διὰ ταῦτα πολὺ μᾶλλον ἢ διὰ Φαρνάβαζον καὶ τὸ χρυσίον
ἐπηρμένοι μισεῖν ᾖ[σ]αν | [35] τοὺς Λακεδαιμονίους.

---

48   παραπλησίως   Grenfell and Hunt.
58   papyrus shows σιχιον. Σι⟨μιχ⟩ον
     Fuhr.
60   [αι ναῦς ἃς ἐπ] Boissevain. [αι
     πλοῖα ἃ ἐπ] Grenfell and Hunt.
61   [τὰς ἕνδεκα] Wilamowitz; [τὰς
     (ἁ)πάσας] Lipsius, Castiglioni.

hated them in Athens were the people who desired to turn the Athenians from tranquillity and peace and lead them towards war and a vigorous policy, so that it might be possible for them to obtain money from the public treasury.

VII.3   Of the Corinthians who wished to bring about a change of policy, most, <like> the Argives and Boeotians, were hostile towards the Spartans, but Timolaus alone was opposed to them on private grounds. Formerly he had been very well-disposed and an outstanding pro-Spartan, as can be learnt from the events of the Decelean War.

VII.4   For having obtained a force of five ships he ravaged some of the islands on the side of the Athenians. And having sailed to Amphipolis with two triremes and manned from there another four in addition, he defeated Simichus, the Athenian general, in a sea-fight, as I have said earlier, and he captured five enemy triremes and thirty vessels which they had sent. Afterwards with ... triremes he sailed to Thasos and caused it to revolt from the Athenians.

VII.5   So it was for these reasons much more than on account of Pharnabazus and the gold that those in aforementioned cities had been incited to hate the Spartans.

VIII (III) Ὁ δὲ Μίλων ὁ τῆς Αἰγ[ί]νης ἁρμοστή[ς,] ὡς ἤκουσε τὰ παρὰ τῶν Ἀθην[αί]ων, συμπληρωσάμενος τριήρη διὰ ταχέω[ν] ἐδίωκε τὸν Δημαίνετον. ὁ δὲ κατὰ τοῦτον τ[ὸν] χρόνον ἔτυχε μὲν ὢν περὶ Θορικὸν τῆς Ἀτ|⁴⁰τικῆς **2** ἔ[πει]δὴ δὲ προσπλεύσας ἐκεῖν[ο]ς πρὸ[ς ‖ . . . . . .] 70 ἐπεχείρη[σεν . . . . .]ειν, ὥρμησεν ἐπὶ πολυ|[. . . . .]ειν· κρατήσ[ας δὲ μιᾶς ν]εὼς αὐτῶν τὴν μὲν ὑ|[φ' αὑτῷ] ναῦν, ὅτι χε[ῖρον ἦν τὸ σκ]άφος, αὐτοῦ κατέλ[ιπ]εν, | [εἰς δὲ] τὴν ἐκείν[ων μεταβιβ]άσας τοὺς αὐτοῦ ναύ|⁵[τας πρ]οέπλ[ε]υσεν [ἐπὶ τὸ στρά]τευμα τὸ μετὰ τοῦ | [Κόνωνος. οὐδὲν δὲ πράξας ὁ Μίλ]ων εἰς Αἴγιναν με|[τὰ τῆς αὐτοῦ νεὼς ἐπανῆκε.

IX (IV) Τὰ μ]ὲν οὖν ἁδρότατα τῶν | [κατὰ τὴν Ἑλλάδα τῷ χειμῶν]ι τούτῳ συμβάντων | [οὕτως ἐγένετο· ἀρχομένου] δὲ τοῦ [θ]έρους τῇ μὲν | ¹⁰[. . . . .] ἔτος ὄγδοον ἐνειστήκει | [. . . . . 80 . . . . .]ορος τὰς τριήρεις απα|[. ἐ]κεῖ δὲ καταπλεύσας τὰς | [. . . . .]εν, ἔτυχεν γὰρ αἰεὶ του|[. . . . . κατεσ]κευακὼς ἦν νεώρια | ¹⁵[. . . . .

---

69 μὲν ὢν Boissevain; μένων Grenfell and Hunt.
70 προ[ς Θορικὸν] ἐπεχειρη[σεν ἐμβαλ]εῖν Grenfell and Hunt; προ[ς τὴν γῆν] ἐπεχειρη[σεν ἐξωθ]εῖν Boissevain.
72 [ας δὲ μιᾶς ν]:[ας δὲ τῆς ν] Wilamowitz; [ας δ'ἐκεῖ ν] Boissevain.
74 πα]ρέπλ[ε]υσεν Richards. [οὐδὲν δὲ πράξας] Castiglioni, *exempli gratia*.
78 τοῦτο Grenfell and Hunt[1].
81 ἀπα[γαγὼν Fuhr; ἁπά[σας? Jacoby.

VIII.1   Milon the harmost of Aegina, on hearing the news from the Athenians, quickly manned a trireme and pursued Demaenetus. He at this time was near Thoricus in Attica.

VIII.2   When he sailed against ... and attempted ... (Demainetus) rushed ... Having seized one of their ships, he left there his own ship because the hull was in a poorer condition. Having transferred his sailors to their ship, he sailed off to the force with Conon. Having achieved nothing, Milon returned with his ship to Aegina.

IX.1   This was the course of the most important events occurring in the Greek world in this winter. At the beginning of the summer ... the eighth year began

.....]ς ὅπου συνέπιπτεν | [..................
...] τὸν δὲ Φαρνάβαζον α|[..................
...] παραγενέσθαι βουλό|[μενος..............
..]αι καὶ μισθὸν ἀπολα|[βεῖν................ **2** ..].ος
μὲν οὖν αὐτοῦ διε|[20][......, ἐπὶ δὲ τὰς ναῦς τῶν Λακ]ε-
δαιμονίων καὶ τῶν | [συμμάχων ἀφικνεῖται Πόλλις] ναύ- 90
αρχος ἐκ Λακε|[δαίμονος εἰς τὴν ναυαρχίαν τὴ]ν Ἀρχε-
λαΐδα κατα|[στὰς διάδοχος. κατὰ δὲ τὸν αὐ]τὸν χρόνον
Φοινίκων |[καὶ Κιλίκων ἧκον ἐνενήκοντ]α νῆες εἰς Καῦνον,
ὧν | [25][δέκα μὲν ἔπλευσαν ἀπὸ Κιλι]κίας, αἱ δὲ λείπουσαι |
[.........................]ας αὐτῶν ὁ Σιδώνιος |
[δυνάστης........ βασ]ιλεῖ τοῖς ταύτης τῆς |
[χώρας......... πε]ρὶ τὴ[ν] ναυαρχίαν. Φαρ-|
[νάβαζος............]ντων αὐτὸν τῶν παρα|
[30][...................]. αρος τὰ περὶ τὴν ἀρχὴν |
[............ τὸ στρατό]πεδον. **3** Κ[ό]νων δὲ 100
προσ|[........... αἰ]σθόμενος ἀναλα-
βὼν | [........... καὶ συμ]πληρώσας τὰς τριήρεις |
[............ ὡς τάχι]στα ποταμ[ὸ]ν τὸν Καύ-|
[35][νιον καλούμενον εἰς λίμνη]ν τὴν Κ[α]υνίαν εἰσέπλευ|[σε
.... το]ῦ Φαρναβάζου καὶ τοῦ Κό|[νω-
νος............ φέ]ρνη[ς] ἀνὴρ Πέρσης πα|[..
............] τῶν πραγμάτων, ὃς | [.....
.... ἠβ]ούλετο λαβ[ε]ῖν [κ]ατα|[40][.....
........].ν δὲ πρ[.].[...]ν[.]με[..]ν φιλ[ί]αν | [...

---

93 [παρεγενήθησαν ἐνενήκοντ]α Meyer.
95 αὐτῶν Bartoletti (P.McK's observations
support this); Ἄκτων Grenfell and Hunt[1].
104 καλούμενον Bury.
106 Πασιφέ]ρνη[ς] or Ἀρταφέ]ρνη[ς]
(Compare D.S. XIV.79.5).

IX.2   ... but Pollis came from Sparta to the fleet of the Spartans and their allies as admiral, in succession to the command of Archelaidas. About the same time 90 ships of the Phoenicians and Cilicians came to Caunus, of which ten had sailed from Cilicia, and the remainder ... ... of them the Sidonian ruler ...

IX.3   and, having manned the triremes ... as quickly as possible he sailed up the river called the Caunian, into the Caunian lake ... of Pharnabazus and Conon ... −phernes a Persian man ... sent [him?] to the King ...

. . . .].ος ἀπέπεμψεν ὡ[ς] βασιλέα σ[. . .]α|[. 110
. . . . . . τ]ὴν σκηνὴν αὐτοῦ . [. . . . . .]ἦλθ[ε . .]ν|[. . . .
. . . . . ἀ]παγγείλας δὲ τὰ π[. . . . .]εασᾳ[. .]ν ‖

desunt versus XXV

| **X** (V) ^{26}.[- - -] | .[- - -]|α[- - -]|φε[- - -]||^{30}α.
[- - -]|π[- - -]|β . [- - -]|τα[. .]τα[- - -]|ποντα [- - -] |
^{35}ἀρχ[ο]ντ[- - -]|κους ἰστ[- - -]|σιν τὰς μ[- - -] | [.]ωσιν
πρ[- - -]|[. .]τεκελ[- - -]|^{40}νων οὐδ[- - -] | ἔχοντες
[- - -] | εἶχον γὰ[ρ . . .

B

XI (VI) - -], εἰσὶν δὲ κα[. . . |. . . . .
. . . . τῶ]ν ἱππέων [. . . |. . . . .
. . . .], ἔνιοι δὲ πρ[. . . | 120
. . . .]στιον. ἡ μὲν [οὖν | ^{5}. . . . .
. . . .] τοιαύτῃ κ[. .]ι[. | . . . .
. . . .]ις. **2** Ἀγησίλα[ος] δὲ | [. . . . .
. . . . τὸ] στρατόπ[ε]δον, | [. . . . .
. . . . τὸ] Κα[ΰσ]τρι|[ον πεδίον . . . . .
. . . .] τὰ ὄρη τῳξάμε|^{10}[νος . . . .
. . . .]ους, ταύτῃ πάλιν | [. . . . .
. . . .]ης τοιαύτῃ φθά|[σας . . . .
. . . .]ς τὸ στρατόπεδον | [. . . . .

---

118 The work of the second scribe begins at
this line.
121 προά[στιον Fuhr.
124 There is a punctuation mark in the
papyrus after στρατόπ[ε]δον.
126 [νος εἰς πλινθίον? Grenfell and Hunt[1].

XI.2 ... the plain] of the Ca[ys]ter ....

....]ειν. 3 Τισσαφέρ[ν]ης | [................ 130
ἐπηκο]λούθει τοῖς Ἕλλη[σ]ιν|¹⁵[............ ἱππέας
μὲν ... α]κισχιλίους κα[ὶ] μυ|[ρίους, πεζοὺς δὲ ....
μυρίων ο]ὐκ ἐλάττους. | [Ἀγησίλαος δὲ ....
ἡγη]σάμενος χαλε|[πὸν προσβάλλοντας τοὺς πολεμίο]υς
ἐκ παρατά|[ξεως ἀμύνεσθαι πολὺ τῶν Ἑλλήνων ὑ]περέ-
χοντας, | ²⁰[................................]λως
καὶ κρα|[τ.................................] στρα-
τηγίας | [...............................]σαντα μά-
χεσθαι | [................................]ων στρατευ-
μα|[...................................]σας, οἱ δὲ βάρ- 140
βα|²⁵[ροι................................]ες καὶ συν-
τετα|[γμέν...............................] ἔχοντες το-
σου|[τ...............................δ]υνατὸς ἀφορ-
μᾶν | [...............................κα]τεῖδον τοὺς
Ἕλλη|[νας.............................ο]ὔτε τὴν πο-
ρείαν | ³⁰[................................] κατα-
φρονεῖν | [...............................]ντες αὐ-

---

130 There is a punctuation mark in the
papyrus after]ειν.
131-3 πεζοὺς μὲν πεντα]κισχιλίους
κα[ὶ] μυ[ρίους ἔχων, ἱππέας δὲ
μυρίων ο]ὐκ ἐλάττους Wilamowitz;
πεντακισμυρίων ο]ὐκ ἐλάττους
Grenfell and Hunt.
135 There is a punctuation mark in the
papyrus after ὑ]περέχοντας.
140 There is a punctuation mark in the
papyrus after]σας.
147]ντες: the ε is written above a letter α
as a correction.

XI.3 Tissaphernes ... followed the Greeks ... [14–19,000] cavalry and not less than [multiple of 10,000] infantry. But Agesilaus, thinking it difficult to resist the enemy attacking in battle array, since they were more numerous than the Greeks ...

τοὺς | [..........................] τοῦ στρα-
τεύ|[ματος ....] προσβαλόν-|
[τ........................ἔξ]ωθεν τοῦ πλιν|³⁵[θίου   150
..........................]ον προσέτατ|[τε......
..................], τοὺς δὲ Πελοπον|[νησίους καὶ
τοὺς συμμάχους....]ι προσῆγε πρ||[........
............ὡς] ἑώρα τοὺς Ἕλλη|[νας........
..........]λεον α[..]ων ἀεὶ | ⁴⁰[..........
..............ὁ]μοίως, ε[..]διε||[..........
........]ν ἐγγυτέρω μᾶλ|λο[ν..........
....οὐ]δὲν ἀλλ' ἢ τὸν | ποτ[αμὸν..........
...] γὰρ ἀμφοτερ[..] | ηγ[..........
...]ετ[.] προιόν[τ..] | ⁴⁵δε[..........   160
... ὀ]λίγ[...]σ[.....]|ει[..........
στρα]τευμ[α.......] | τε[..........
..]αν[....]..4 Ἀ[γησί]|λα[ος δὲ..........
..........]. ν[..]||τ[..........
στρ]ατ[ε]υμα[...| ⁵⁰..........
...]ιπονο[...
π]αρασκευα[..]|.[..........]ιους
ἵνα τῇ ν.[...|.......κα]τα-
[ν]έμουσι[....] | κα[..................]
ωνην πολλ[..] | ⁵⁵ α[.................] 170
βουλευσομ[εν..] | π.[............]ν
τὸν ενια.[...] | οι.[............]
νοιτινεια[...] | ε.[.........ο]υς
ἔγνω κα.[..]|ο.[............]
.των τῆς νυκτ[ὸς] | ⁶⁰.ι[

---

156 There is a punctuation mark in the
    papyrus after]μοίως.
161 δ in the left hand margin, probably
    indicating the 400th line.

μὲν] ὁπλίτας, [πεν]|| τακοσίους δ[ὲ ψ]ιλούς, καὶ το[ύτοις
ἐπέστησεν ἄρχοντα] Ξενοκλέα [Σ]παρτιάτην, π[αραγγείλας
ὅταν γένωνται] βαδίζοντε[ς] κατ' αὐτοὺς [. . . . .
. . . .] εἰς μάχην τ[άττ]εσθαι. [. . . . .
. . . . . .]χ[. .] | ⁵ἀναστήσας ἅ[μα τῇ ἡμ]έρᾳ [τ]ὸ ͺστͺρά[τε]υ̣- 180
[μα πάλιν] ἀνῆγεν εἰς τὸ πρ[όσθεν. οἱ] δὲ βάρβαροι
συνα[κολουθήσ]αντες ὡς εἰώθεσα[ν οἱ μὲ]ν αὐτῶν προσέ-
βαλλ[ον] τοῖς Ἕλλησιν, οἱ δὲ πε[ρίιππε]υον αὐτούς, οἱ δὲ
κ[α]τὰ τὸ πεδίον ἀτάκτ[ως ἐπ]ηκολούθουν. 5 ὁ δὲ Ξ[ε]-
νοκλῆς, | ¹⁰ἐπειδὴ καιρ[ὸν ὑπ]έλαβεν εἶναι τοῖς πολεμίοις
ἐπιχειρεῖν, ἀνα[στήσ]ας ἐκ τῆς ἐνέδρας τοὺς Πελοπον-
νησίους ἔ{ω}θ[ει δρ]όμῳ· τῶν δὲ βαρβάρων ὡς εἶδον
ἕκαστοι προσθέ[ον]τας τοὺς Ἕλληνας ἔφευγον καθ'
ἅπαν τὸ πεδίον. Ἀγ[ησίλ]αος δὲ κατιδὼν πεφοβημένους
αὐ|¹⁵τοὺς ἔπεμπεν ἀπὸ τοῦ στρατεύματος τούς τε κούφους 190
[τ]ῶν στρατιωτῶν καὶ τοὺς ἱππέας διώξοντας ἐκείνους·
οἱ δὲ μετὰ τῶν ἐκ τῆς ἐνέδρας ἀναστάντ⟨ων⟩ ἐνέκειντο
τ⟨οῖς⟩ βαρβάρ⟨οις⟩. 6 ἐπακολουθήσαντες δὲ τοῖς πολεμί-
[ο]ις οὐ λίαν πολὺ[ν] χρόνον, οὐ γὰρ [ἠδύ]ναντο κατα-
λαμβά|²⁰νειν {ε}αὐτοὺς ἅτε τ[ῶ]ν πολλῶν [ἱππ]έων ὄν-
των καὶ γυμνήτων, καταβάλλουσιν μὲν [αὐ]τῶν περὶ
ἑξακοσίους, ἀποστάντες δὲ τῆς διώ[ξεω]ς ἐβ[ά]δ[ι]ζον

---

176 The three possibilities are
[πεν]|τακοσίους, [ἐπ]|τακοσίους and
[ὀκ]|τακοσίους. At the end of the last
line of column 5 after ὁπλίτας[there is
a space for up to three letters.
179 There is a punctuation mark in the
papyrus after]εσθαι.
183 πε[ρίιππε]υον Boissevain.
192 The papyrus reads ἀνάσταντες.
193 The papyrus reads τῶν βαρβάρων.

62

XI.4 ... hoplites and ... hundred light-armed troops, and made Xenocles, a Spartiate, their commander, having ordered that when the Persians happened to be coming against them ... draw up for battle ... Agesilaus roused up his army at dawn and again led it forward. Having followed as they had been accustomed to do, some of the barbarians attacked the Greeks, others rode around them, and others began to pursue them across the plain in an undisciplined fashion. XI.5 When he judged it the right moment to attack the enemy, Xenocles roused the Peloponnesians from their ambush and charged at the double. When the barbarians saw the Greeks charging at them, they fled fled all over the plain. Seeing them terrified, Agesilaus sent the light-armed troops of his army and the cavalry to pursue them. Together with those who had come from the ambush, they fell upon the barbarians.

XI.6 They chased the enemy but not for very long, for they could not catch them because the majority were cavalry and troops without armour. They killed about six hundred of them, then they broke off the pursuit and

ἐπ' αὐτὸ τὸ στρατόπεδον τὸ τῶν βα[ρβάρ]ων. [κα]ταλα-
βόντες δὲ φυλακὴν οὐ σπουδαί[ως κ]αθε[στῶ]σαν ταχέ-|
²⁵ως αἱροῦσιν, κα[ὶ] λαμβάνουσιν [α]ὐτῶν [πολ]λὴν μὲν 200
ἀγοράν, συχνο[ὺς] δὲ ἀνθρώπο[υ]ς, πολλ[ὰ δὲ] σκεύη καὶ
χρήματα ⟨τὰ⟩ μὲν [τῶ]ν ἄλλων τὰ δ[ὲ] Τισσαφέ[ρνους]
αὐτοῦ.

XII (VII) Γενομένης δὲ τ[ῆς] μάχης τοιαύ[τ]ης οἱ μὲ[ν
βά]ρβαροι καταπλαγέντες [τοὺς] Ἕλληνας ἀπεχώρησ[αν
σὺν] τῷ Τισ[³⁰σαφέρνει πρὸς τὰς Σάρδεις· Ἀγησίλαος δὲ
περ[ιμε]ίνας αὐτοῦ τρεῖς ἡμέρας, ἐν αἷς τοὺς νεκροὺς
ὑποσπ[όν]δους ἀπέδωκεν τοῖς π[ο]λεμίοις καὶ τροπαῖον
ἔστη[σε] καὶ τὴν γῆν ἅπασαν ἐ[πόρθ]ησεν, προῆγεν τὸ
στρ[άτε]υμα εἰς Φρυγίαν πάλιν [τὴν] μεγάλην. **2** ἐποιεῖτο
δὲ [τ]ὴν πορείαν | ³⁵οὐκέτι συντεταγμένους ἔχων ἐν τῷ 210
πλ[ι]νθίῳ τοὺς στρατιώτας, ἀλλ' ἐῶν αὐτοὺς ὅσην
ἠβούλοντο τῆς χώρας ἐπιέναι καὶ κακῶς ποιε[ῖν τοὺς]
πολεμ[ί]ους. Τισσαφέρνης δὲ πυθόμενος τοὺς [Ἕλληνας
β]αδίζειν εἰς τὸ πρόσθε⟨ν⟩ ἀναλαβὼν αὖθις τοὺς β[αρ-
βάρους ἐ]πη[κολο]ύθει ὄπισθεν | ⁴⁰αὐτῶν πολλοὺς σταδίο[υς
διέχων. **3** Ἀγ]ησίλ[αος] δὲ διεξελθ[ὼν] τὸ πε[δ]ίον τὸ
τῶν Λυδῶν [ἦγε τὴν στρ]ατιὰν [......] διὰ τῶ[ν] ὀρῶν
τῶν διὰ μέσου κε[ιμένων τῆ]ς τ[ε Λυδίας] καὶ τῆς Φρυγίας·
ἐπειδὴ δὲ διεπορ[εύθησαν ταῦτα, κατεβίβ]ασε τοὺς
Ἕλληνας εἰς τὴν Φ[ρυγίαν, ἕως ἀφίκοντο πρὸς τ]ὸν | 220

---

203 The work of the first scribe begins again here.
214 The papyrus reads πρόσθε, but at a line—end.
217 [ἀμαχεὶ] διὰ Wilamowitz; [ἀσφαλῶς] διὰ Fuhr.

went to the camp of the barbarians. Taking the garrison, which was not well organised, by surprise, they seized the camp speedily and captured lots of supplies, many men and much equipment and money, some belonging to others, some to Tissaphernes himself.

XII.1   This being the nature of the battle, the barbarians, terrified by the Greeks, moved away with Tissaphernes to Sardis.

Agesilaus, having waited there three days (in which he returned to the enemy their dead under truce, set up a trophy, and ravaged the entire area), then once again led his force forward to Greater Phrygia.   XII.2 He made the journey no longer having his soldiers drawn up in square formation but allowing them to attack what land they wanted and to cause harm to the enemy. Perceiving that the Greeks were advancing, Tissaphernes, once again taking the barbarians with him, followed behind them, keeping many stades distance.

XII.3   Journeying through the plain of Lydia, Agesilaus led the army ... through the mountains lying between Lydia and Phrygia. When they had crossed these, he brought the Greeks down to Phrygia until they reached the Maeander

⁴⁵Μαίανδρον ποταμόν, ὃ[ς ἔχει μὲν τὰς πηγὰς ἀπὸ Κελαι-]
νῶν, ἣ τῶν ἐν Φρυγίᾳ μεγίστη [πόλις ἐστίν, ἐκδίδωσι δ']
εἰς θάλατταν παρὰ Πριήνην κ[αὶ .... 4 καταστρα-]
τοπεδεύσας δὲ τοὺς Πελοπ[οννησίους καὶ τοὺς σ]υμμάχους
ἐθύετο πότ[ερ]α χ[ρὴ] δ[ι]αβ[αίνειν τὸν ποτ]α|⁵⁰μὸν ἢ μή,
καὶ βαδίζειν ἐπὶ Κελα[ινὰς ἢ πάλιν το]ὺς στρατιώτας
ἀπάγειν. ὡς δὲ συνέβ[αινεν αὐτῷ] μὴ γίγνεσθαι καλὰ τὰ
ἱερά, περιμε[ί]να[ς ἐκεῖ τήν τ]ε ἡμέραν ἣν παρεγένετο καὶ
τὴν ἐπιο[ῦσαν ἀπῆγ]εν τὸν ‖ [στρατὸν ....
Ἀγησί]λαος μὲν οὖ[ν ... | .... τὸ πεδίον τὸ 230
Μαιάν]δρου καλούμενο[ν] | δ[..............
....]. νέμονται Λυδ[οὶ] | κ[αὶ ....
.... XIII (VIII) ...]. δὲ βασιλεὺς | ⁵.[...........
.... π]ερὶ τούτους | τ[.............
.... στρ]ατηγόν, ἅμα | δὲ [.............
............]. Τισσαφέρνῃ | ετ[.............
.... το]ὺς Ἕλληνας | μ.[.............
............]νουν καὶ μᾶλ|¹⁰λο[ν ....
............]. δίχα κει|με[ν ....
..........................]|εξ[.......... 240
..........................] | συ[............
Τισσ]αφ[έρν ....]|οπ[...........
Ἀρταξ]έρξ[.................] | ¹⁵δια[..........
......]απαρ[................] | λο[..........
....]κα[..]οιτε[.....]. σα[..........]|οργ[....

---

221 ἔχει μὲν τὰς πηγὰς ἀπὸ Κελαι]νῶν
    Lipsius.
222 ἐκδίδωσι δ'] Lipsius; ἐκδίδωσιν]
    Grenfell and Hunt.
237 μ. Bartoletti.
244 Παρ[ύσατις ? Meyer.

66

River which takes its source from Celaenae which is the greatest city in Phrygia, and flows out to the sea near Priene and ...

XII.4   Having encamped the Peloponnesians and their allies, he made a sacrifice to find out whether he should cross the river or not, whether to march against Celaenae or to lead his army back again. Since it happened that the sacrifices were not auspicious, he waited there the day on which he arrived and the following day, then withdrew his army ... So Agesilaus ... the plain of the Maeander ... there live the Lydians and ...

........] αὐτῷ κατηγ[.] . α[.]αδι[..........]|ͅσα
[...]τε βασιλεὺς ὁμολογουγτ̣[. .] μάλιστ̣[α ....] |
δι[ὰ Τισ]σαφέρνην καὶ πα[.] . γ ἐκεῖνον [...........]|
²⁰πάντων καθ᾿ ἃ Τιθρα[ύστης α]ὑτὸν κα[.]. [........
...] ͅ ὃς ἐπειδὴ καταφ[..... Φρυ]γίαν καὶ Λυδ[ίαν 250
.......]|το[....]εν ἀνέπεμψ[εν ἐπιστ]ολὰς ἃς ἔφε-
ρ[ε..........]|ρα[......]ι πρὸς Ἀρι[αῖον Τι]σσαφ[έ]ρ-
νη[..........] | ἐπ[.....]ο πρὸς Με̣.[..]αιον ὡς
α.[...........]|²⁵στ.[....] λαβεῖν ἐκελ̣[...]
αιδ[................] | εὐ[......]υτου γε[...]
ται [................]|πε[......]νουτο[....]
ον[................]|λω[.......].ν ἔ[μ]ελλεν
ηχ[.............] | σιν[........ Τ]ιθραύ-
σ[τ.............]|³⁰τα.[........]τ[...
...............]δε|δο.[........ 260
...........]της | ἀποκρε[........
...........] η̣[..]|ρίζεσθ[αι........
...........] | ὁπότε α̣[........
...........] Τισσα]|³⁵φέρνη[ν ἀ]πέστειλεν τ̣[....
....]ο̣α̣ρ[........]ο̣ | Ἀρ[ι]α[ῖ]ος εἰς Σάρδεις
το[........]ονου[....... δυ]|νατὸς Τισσαφέρ-

---

246 Not space for κατηγ[ορί]α: Grenfell and Hunt.
253 ἐπ[έμψατ]ο Grenfell and Hunt¹.
254 ἐκελ̣ευσε or ἐκεῖ[or ἐκεῖ[νον could be read: Grenfell and Hunt.

• • • • •

νη[. . . . .] . ρια . [. . . . .] | βέλτιστοι τῶν
στρ[ατη]γῷ[ν . .]. ιανετε .[. . . . ἀκιν]|δυν[ότ]ερον ἕξειν
τ[ὰ κ]ατὰ τή[ν] σα[τ]ραπία[ν Ἀγησιλά]|⁴⁰ου κα[θ]ημένου
περὶ [τ]ὴν Μαγν[η]σ[ί]αν ἐμι[. . . . .] | τῶν [πε]ζῶ[ν] 270
καὶ τῶν ἱππέω[ν . . .]ω προ[. . . . .]|ε[. . .]ον δ[ια-]
κειμένου[. ἀλ]|λ[ο]υς ἄλλη
ποι[. .].αν[. . . . .] | βουλόμενος
δ[. .]π[.].[. . . . .] | ⁴⁵στράτευμα
τα[.].[. . . . .] || **2** [- - -] | [- - -] | [. . . .]ν[-
- -] | [. . .]προ[- - -]|⁵π' Ἀρταξ[έρξ - - -]|τα ἡμέρα[ς
- - -] | αὐτὸν α[- - - Φρυ]|γίας ἐπια[- - -] | τὸν Τι-
θρ[αύστην - - - Τισσα]|¹⁰φέρνης [- - -] | πρᾶξιν α[- - -
οἰ]|κοδομε[ῖν - - -] | πόλεως .[- - -] | ὑπὸ τῶν [- - -]
¹⁵.εβαδ[ι - - -] | τῷ Τιθρα[ύστη - - -]|σ[.]αι παρα[- 280
- -] | ἐπιστολὰ[ς - - -] | πρὸς τὴν α[- - -]|²⁰τιας κατα.[-
- -]|.ε Μιλη[σι - - -]|ψας καὶ τα.[- - - κα]|τῆρεν
εἰς [- - -] | Ἀριαῖον ε[- - - με]|²⁵τὰ δὲ ταῦ[τα - - -]
διατρίβω[ν - - -] | ἱμάτια τ[- - -]|νον συναρ[πα - - -]
καὶ μεταπ[- - -] | ³⁰[. .]λοι.ν ἱπ[π - - -] | συνεχ[- - -]
μεν.[- - -]|τησδ[- - -] | ἔλεγ[ε - - -]|³⁵τ[ο]ν βα[σιλ]έως
[- - -] | τα[ῖ]ς ἐπιστολ[αῖς - - -]|[. .]ε τὸ βυβλ[ίον -
- -] | [. .]ττεν βασιλ[ε - - -] | [. .] αὐτὸν ἀνα[- - -]

---

267 Ἀριαι̣[Grenfell and Hunt¹ (doubtfully)
Ἀριαῖ[ος δὲ καὶ οἱ] βέλτιστοι Kalinka.
270 Grenfell and Hunt called Μαγν[η]σ[ί]αν 'not
very satisfactory': P. McK's observations suggest
Μαγν̣[η]σ[ίαν].
ἐμι[σθώσαντο δὲ] τῶν Kalinka.
276 ἐπ]τὰ or τριάκον]τα Grenfell and Hunt¹.
284 λουόμε]νον or γυμ]νὸν Grenfell and Hunt¹.
288 καθὼς προσέτα]ττεν βασιλ̣εύς Wilcken.

XIII.1 ... the best of the generals ... to control matters in his satrapy more securely with Agesilaus camped around Magnesia ... of the infantry and cavalry ...

⁴⁰[..] ... ειν εκ.[- - -] | [ἄ]λλην ἀναγ[- - -] | [τῶ]ν βαρ-
βάρω[ν ...

C

C Col. I   Fr. 8   Fr. 9
desunt versus XV

XIV (IX)]νᾳ[.]   ]καὶ
 ]καγα-   ]λει   π]αραγγει-
πόλ]εμον   ]μφε-   ] καταμα-
 ].ισωτη   ]τατον   ]ν παραλα-
 ]λλην αὐ-   ]κοσι-   ] Μακεδο-

2 ||νοτη[.].ασ[- - -] | ἅμα μὲν [.]ου.[- - -] | ἀφθό[ν]ω[ς
..]σ.[- - -, ἅ]|μα δὲ [γ]ενεσ[- - -] | ⁵ἐπὶ τη. .ιματ[-
- -] | ᾐρημένον ὕπαρξα[- - -] | δι᾽ ἐκειν[...]ητ[.]σ.[-
- -]|[.]αλωνῳ.[- - -]||[τ]ερον πω[- - -] | ¹⁰καὶ βιαζ.
[- - -] | χρόνον μ[- - -] | πολλῆς δυνά[μεως -
- -] | ὁμοί[.]ν α.[.]ο.[.]α[- - -]||κως [.]ην.[.].ε[- - -
ἤτοι]|¹⁵μασεν ἠγε[μ- - -]|.τέρους Ἑλ[λ]η[ν- - -] | ἢ τοὺ[ς
ἐκ τ[ο]ῦ π[ο]λ[έμου] γιγνομ[ένους . . . .]|νος
δὲ τὴν [ἡ]σ[υ]χ[ί]αν ἄριστα τ[οῖς πράγμασι φαίνεται] |
κεχρημέν[ος·] οὐ γὰρ ὥσπερ ο[ἱ πλεῖστοι τῶν πρὸ τοῦ
δυ]|²⁰ναστευόντω[ν] ὥρμησεν ἐ[πὶ τὰς τῶν χρημάτων
ἁρπα]|γάς, καὶ δη[μο]τικώτα[τ]ος τ[. . . . .

---

298 [γ]ενεσ Bartoletti: the traces of εν are not
   discernible to P. McK.
305 [ἡ]σ[υ]χ[ί]αν or [ἁ]τ[υ]χ[ί]αν Grenfell and
   Hunt.
308 δη[μο]τικώτα[τ]ος or δη[μο]τικώτε[ρ]ος
   Grenfell and Hunt; the ink is very indistinct.

XIV.2   ... the peace, he appears to have managed affairs very well; for he did not, like most of the earlier holders of power, go after extortions of money, and ... very democratic ...

```
.....] | μεταπεμπό[μ]ενος ἐκ [.......... τοὺς ....
.....]|κέναι τι δοκ[ο]ῦντας δ[................... 310
.....] | τῶν πλεί[στω]ν χ[......................
.....] | 25[....].[..]ε[...]τ[_
```

Fragmenta Columnae X ut videtur tribuenda

Fr. 10

```
---                    5 των[
[..]ωσ[                 πασα[
ηλωσεν[                 των[
δοξαν [_ _ _  Λα-       ---
κεδα[ιμον
```

Fr. 11

```
    ----
    ]η[
    ] καὶ δει[                     320
    ] . [.]υτω[
    ] . . μι[
    ]ατεδ[
    ] . [.]ελ[
    ]εοτ[
    ]αν ἐκε[
τῶν] ἄλλων βαρβάρω[ν
    ] . [.] ἀλλὰ τὴν με[
    ] . [.]τοῦ δὲ βίον . ιρ . [.]τ[
    ]ς περὶ πολλὴν στ . . . σ[     330
```

---

315 ἀν]ήλωσεν ? Kalinka.

κα]τήγαγεν· ἀντὶ ὧν ἠγα[πημένος
]ς ἐποίησε κατακει[
]λλαις κατασκευα[
] περὶ δὲ τὴν του[

(finis columnae)

Fr. 12

]...[5]των παρ' εκειν[
]. δὲ προστ[   ]αθα περιμε.[
]ων ειλη[   ]ν επιτα[
]. τελευ]τ   ]ιλαθε[

Fr. 13   Fr. 14   Fr. 15

]θ.[   ]ων[   ]μ[
]υτον[   ]ιακα[   ]σε[.]ιο[
]εν αὐτ[   ]τιτ[   ]ας πολ[
]αιρεῖσθ[αι   ]τιδα[   ].[
5].[....]τ[

---
331 ἠγα[πημένος Bartoletti; ἠγα[πᾶτο Meyer.

D

XV (X) - ‖ . . . . .]ς βο[. . . . .
. .] . καθ' ἑκά‖[στην] ἡμέ[ρ]αν ἐξήτ[αζε τοὺς στρατιώτας]
σὺν τοῖς ὅ‖[πλοις] ἐν [τ]ῷ λιμέν[ι, προφασιζόμενος μὲ]ν
ἵνα μὴ ῥᾳ‖[θυμο]ῦντες χείρους [γένωνται πρὸς τὸν] πόλε- 350
μον, βου|[5][λόμε]νος δὲ παρασκε[υάζειν προθύμους] τοὺς
Ῥοδίους [ἐὰν ἴ]δωσιν ἐν τοῖς ὅ[πλοις αὐτοὺς παρόν]τας
τηνικαῦ[τα τοῖ]ς ἔργοις ἐπιχειρε[ῖν· ὡς δὲ σύνηθες
ἅ]πασιν ἐποί[ησεν] ὁρᾶν τὸν ἐξετα[σμόν, αὐτὸς μὲν εἴ]κοσι
λαβὼν [τῶν] τριήρων ἐξέπλευ[σεν εἰς Καῦνον, βου]λόμενος
[10][μὴ π]αρεῖναι τῇ διαφθο[ρᾷ τῶν ἀρχόντω]ν, Ἱερωνύ-
μῳ [δὲ κ]αὶ Νικοφήμῳ προσέ[ταξεν ἐπιμελ]ηθῆναι τῶν
[πρα]γμάτων οὖσιν αὐτοῦ πα[ρέδροις. 2 οἳ π]εριμείναν-
[τες] ἐκείνην τὴν ἡμέραν, π[αρόντων ἐπὶ] τὸν ἐξετα[σμὸ]ν
τῇ ὑστεραίᾳ τῶν στρατι[ωτῶν καθά]περ εἰώθε|[15][σαν,] 360
τοὺς μὲν αὐτῶν παρήγα[γον ἐν τοῖ]ς ὅπλοις εἰς [τὸ]ν λιμένα, τ[ο]ὺς δὲ μικρὸν [ἔξω τῆ]ς ἀγορᾶς. τῶν [δὲ] Ῥοδίων
οἱ συνειδότες τὴν π[ρᾶξιν, ὡ]ς ὑπέλαβον [κ]αιρὸν ἐγχει-
ρεῖν εἶναι τοῖς ἔργ[οις, συ]νελέγοντο [σὺ]ν ἐγχειριδίοις εἰς
τὴν ἀγοράν, καὶ Δωρίμαχος [20][μ]ὲν αὐτῶν ἀναβὰς ἐπὶ

349 The papyrus here show τοις ὁ:
unusually, the rough breathing is
marked.   προφασιζόμενος μὲ]ν
Wilamowitz; πρόφασιν μὲν παρέχω]ν
Rich.
352 ἐὰν ἴ]δωσιν Grenfell and Hunt;   ὅταν
ἴ]δωσιν Wilamowitz.   ὡς δὲ σύνηθες
ἅ]πασιν Fuhr;   ἐπειδὴ συνήθη] πᾶσιν
Wilamowitz.
356 ἀρχόντω]ν Bartoletti; Διαγορείω]ν
Grenfell and Hunt; γνωρίμω]ν Kalinka.
362 ἔξω Bartoletti; ἀπὸ Grenfell and Hunt.

XV.1 Each day he reviewed the soldiers with their weapons at the harbour, the pretext being that they should not become lazy and unfit for the war, but in fact wanting to raise the morale of the Rhodians with the idea that if they saw them there in armour they might engage in action immediately. When he had accustomed them all to seeing the review, he himself took twenty of the triremes and sailed to Caunus, not wanting to be there at the overthrow of the government. He had commanded Hieronymus and Nicophemus, his lieutenants, to take care of the situation.

XV.2 They bided their time during that day, and when the soldiers were there for the review on the following day in the usual fashion, they led some under arms to the harbour and others to just outside the market−place. Those of the Rhodians who were in the know, when they realised it was time to undertake the deed, gathered with daggers in the market−place, and one of them, Dorimachus, got up on the stone where the

20 τὸν λίθον οὗπερ εἰώθει κη[ρύ]ττειν ὁ κῆρυξ, ἀνακραγὼν
ὡς ἠδύνατο μέγιστον '[ἴ]ωμεν, ὦ ἄνδρες' ἔφη 'πολῖται,
ἐπὶ τοὺς τυράννους [τὴ]ν ταχίστην'. οἱ δὲ λοιποὶ βοήσαν-
τος ἐκείνου τὴν [βο]ήθειαν εἰσπηδήσαντες μετ' ἐγχειρι-
δίων εἰς τὰ συν|25[ἑ]δρια τῶν ἀρχόντων ἀποκτείνουσι τούς 370
τε Διαγο[ρε]ίους καὶ τῶν ἄλλων πολιτῶν ἕνδεκα, διαπραξά-
[μ]ενοι δὲ ταῦτα συνῆγον τὸ πλῆθος τὸ τῶν Ῥοδίων [εἰ]ς
ἐκκλησίαν. 3 ἄρτι δὲ συνειλεγμένων αὐτῶν Κόνων ἧκε
πάλιν ἐκ Καύνου μετὰ τῶν τριήρων· οἱ δὲ τὴν | ³⁰σφαγὴν
ἐξεργασάμενοι καταλύσαντες τὴν παροῦσαν πολιτείαν
κατέστησαν δημοκρατίαν, καὶ τῶν πολιτῶν τινας ὀλίγους
φυγάδας ἐποίησαν. ἡ μὲν οὖν ἐπανάστασις ἡ περὶ τὴν
Ῥόδον τοῦτο τὸ τέλος ἔλαβεν.

XVI (XI) Βοιωτοὶ δὲ καὶ Φωκεῖς τούτου τοῦ θέρους
εἰς | ³⁵πόλεμον κατέστησαν. ἐγένοντο δὲ τῆς ἔχθρας αὐτοῖς 380
[α]ἴτιοι μάλιστα τῶν ἐν ταῖς Θήβαις τινές· οὐ γὰρ πολλοῖς
[ἔ]τεσιν πρότερον ἔτυχον εἰς στασιασμὸν οἱ Βοιωτοὶ προ-
ελθόντες. **2** εἶχεν δὲ τὰ πράγματα τότε κα[τὰ τὴ]ν Βοιω-
τίαν οὕτως· ἦσαν καθεστηκυῖαι βουλαὶ [τό]||τε τέττα[ρες
παρ' ἑ]κάστῃ τῶν πόλεων, ὧν οὐ[χ ἅπασι] τοῖς πολ[ίταις
ἐξῆ]ν μετέχειν, ἀ[λλὰ] τοῖς κεκ[τημένοις] πλῆθός τ[ι χρη-
μά]των, τούτων δὲ τῶν βουλῶ[ν κατὰ] μέρος ἑκάσ[τη
προκ]αθημένη καὶ προβουλεύ[ουσα] | ⁵περὶ τῶν π[ραγ-
μά]των εἰσέφερεν εἰς τὰς τρε[ῖς, ὅτι] δὲ δόξε⟨ι⟩ε[ν] ἁπά-
σα[ι]ς τοῦτο κύριον ἐγίγνετο. **3** κ[αὶ τὰ μὲν] ἴδια διετέλουν 390

---

388 προβουλεύ[ουσα Fuhr; προβουλεύ[σασα
    Grenfell and Hunt.
389 The papyrus reads δεδοζενε[: δὲ
    δοζε⟨ι⟩ε[ν] Ernstedt; δ'ἔδοζεν ἐ[ν]
    Grenfell and Hunt.

herald made announcements, and, shouting out as loud as he could, said "Citizens, let's go for the tyrants as quick as we can!". As he was shouting for support, the rest rushed with daggers to the meeting of the magistrates and killed the Diagorean family and eleven of the other citizens, and having done this they gathered the mass of the Rhodians into an assembly, XV.3 and, as soon as they were assembled, Conon came back from Caunus with the triremes. Those who had perpetrated the massacre overthrew the existing constitution and set up a democracy, and made a few of the citizens exiles. So this was the outcome of the revolution in Rhodes.

XVI.1 This summer the Boeotians and the Phocians went to war. Those chiefly responsible for the bad relations between them were some people in Thebes. Not many years previously there had been political conflict in Boeotia. XVI.2 At that time the situation in Boeotia was as follows. There were four councils established at that time in each of the cities. Not all the citizens were allowed to share in these, but only those with a certain level of wealth. Each of these councils in turn sat and deliberated about policy, and referred it to the other three. What seemed acceptable to all of them was approved.

οὕτω διοικούμενοι, τὸ δὲ τῶ[ν Βοι]ωτῶν τοῦτον ἦν τὸν τρόπον συντεταγμένον. [καθ᾽ ἕν]δεκα μέρη διῄρηντο πάντες οἱ τὴν χώραν οἰκοῦν[τες,] | [10] καὶ τούτων ἕκαστον ἕνα παρείχετο βοιώταρχον [οὕτω·] Θηβαῖοι μὲν τέτταρα⟨ς⟩ συνεβάλλοντο, δύο μὲν ὑπὲ[ρ τῆς] πόλεως, δύο δὲ ὑπὲρ Πλαταιέων καὶ Σκώλου καὶ Ἐρ[υ]θρῶ[ν] καὶ Σκαφῶν καὶ τῶν ἄλλων χωρίων τῶν πρότερον μὲν ἐκείνοις συμπολιτευομένων, τότε δὲ συντε [15] λούντων εἰς τὰς Θήβας. δύο δὲ παρείχοντο βοιωτάρχας Ὀρχομένιοι καὶ Ὑσιαῖοι, δύο δὲ Θεσπιεῖς σὺν Εὐτρήσει καὶ Θίσβαις, ἕνα δὲ Ταναγραῖοι, 400 καὶ πάλιν ἕτερον Ἁλιάρτιοι καὶ Λεβαδεῖς καὶ Κορωνεῖς, ὃν ἔπεμπε κατὰ μέρος ἑκάστη τῶν πόλεων, τὸν αὐτὸν δὲ τρόπον ἐ| [20] βάδιζεν ἐξ Ἀκραιφνίου καὶ Κωπῶν καὶ Χαιρωνείας. 4 οὕτω μὲν οὖν ἔφερε τὰ μέρη τοὺς ἄρχοντας· παρείχετο δὲ καὶ βουλευτὰς ἑξήκοντα κατὰ τὸν βοιώταρχον, καὶ τούτοις αὐτοὶ τὰ καθ᾽ ἡμέραν ἀνήλισκον. ἐπετέτακτο δὲ καὶ στρατιὰ ἑκάστῳ μέρει περὶ χιλίους μὲν | [25] ὁπλίτας, ἱππέας δὲ ἑκατόν· ἁπλῶς δὲ δηλῶσαι κατὰ τὸν ἄρχοντα καὶ τῶν κοινῶν ἀπέλανον καὶ τὰς ε[ἰ]σφορὰς ἐποιοῦντο καὶ δικασ⟨τὰς⟩ ἔπεμπον καὶ μετεῖχον ἁπάντων ὁμοίως 410 καὶ τῶν κακῶν καὶ τῶν ἀγαθῶν. τὸ μὲν οὖν ἔθνος ὅλον οὕτως ἐπολιτεύετο, καὶ τὰ συνέδρια | [30] {καὶ} τὰ κοινὰ τῶν Βοιωτῶν ἐν τῇ Καδμείᾳ συνεκάθιζεν.

---

400 The papyrus reads εὐτρήσι.

XVI.3   They continued to run their internal affairs in this way, but Boeotian affairs were managed in the following way. All who lived in that area were arranged in eleven divisions and each of these provided a Boeotarch as follows. Thebes contributed four (two for the city, two for Plataea, Scolus, Erythrae, Scaphae, and the other places previously linked to them in one political entity but at that time subject to Thebes); Orchomenus and Hysiae provided two Boeotarchs; Thespiae with Eutresis and Thisbae provided two; Tanagra one; and Haliartus, Lebadea and Coronea provided another whom each of the cities sent in turn; and in the same way one came from Acraephnium, Copae and Chaeronea. XVI.4 In this way the divisions returned their magistrates. They provided sixty councillors per Boeotarch and they paid their daily expenses. For the organisation of the army, each division had to provide about one thousand hoplites and one hundred cavalry. To put it simply, depending on the number of its magistrates, each community shared in the common treasury, paid its taxes, appointed jurymen, and shared equally in public burdens and benefits. This was the constitution of the whole people, and the council and the common assemblies of the Boeotians sat in the Cadmea.

XVII (XII) Ἐν δὲ ταῖς Θήβαις ἔτυχον οἱ βέλτιστοι καὶ γνωριμώτατοι τῶν πολιτῶν, ὥσπερ καὶ πρότερον εἴρηκα, στασιάζοντες πρὸς ἀλλήλους. ἡγοῦντο δὲ τοῦ μέρους τοῦ μὲν Ἰσμηνίας κα[ὶ] Ἀντίθεος καὶ Ἀνδροκλ⟨είδα⟩ς, | ³⁵τοῦ δὲ Λεοντιάδης καὶ Ἀσίας καὶ Κο⟨ιρα⟩τάδας, ἐφρόνουν δὲ τῶν πολιτευομένων οἱ μὲν περὶ τὸν Λεοντιάδην τὰ Λακεδαιμονίων, [ο]ἱ δὲ περὶ τὸν Ἰσμηνίαν αἰτίαν μὲν εἶχον 420 ἀττικίζειν, ἐξ ὧν πρόθυμοι πρὸς τὸν δῆμον ἐγένοντο ὡς ἔφυγ⟨ε⟩ν· οὐ μὴν ἐφρόν‖[τιζον] τῷ[ν Ἀ]θηναίων, ἀλλ' εἶχ[ον.............].. π[......]έσχον, ἐπεὶ του[................]... πρ[οη]ροῦντο μᾶλ-λ[ον..............]ες κακῶς ποιεῖν ἑτοίμους α[..........|⁵...ἱ]ζειν. **2** διακε[ιμ]ένων δὲ τῶν ἐν [ταῖς Θή]βαις οὕ|τω κ]αὶ τῆς ἑταιρείας ἑκατ[έρ]ας ἰσχ[νούσης....]τα|[..πρ]οῆλθον πολλοὶ καὶ τῶν ἐν ταῖς [πόλεσι ταῖς κ]α|[τὰ τὴ]ν Βοιωτίαν κα[ὶ] μετέ[σ]χον ἑκ[ατέρας τῶν ἑ|ταιρει]ῶν ἐκείνοις. ἐδύναντο δὲ τ[ότε μὲν καὶ 430 ἔτι | ¹⁰μικ]ρῷ πρότερον οἱ πε[ρ]ὶ τὸν Ἰσμη[νίαν καὶ τὸ]ν | [Ἀνδ]ροκλείδ⟨α⟩ν καὶ παρ' αὐτοῖς τοῖ[ς Θηβαίοις κ]αὶ |

---

417 The papyrus reads Ἀνδροκλῆς here, but [Ἀνδ]ροκλείδην at 17.2 and Ἀνδροκλείδαν at 18.1 and 3.

418 The papyrus reads Ἀσίας here, but Ἀστίαν at 17.2.

422 The papyrus reads ἔφυγον: ἔφυγ⟨ε⟩ν Wilamowitz.

426 ἀττικί]ζειν Grenfell and Hunt; λακωνί]ζειν Kalinka.

428 ἔπει]τα Grenfell and Hunt; πλεῖσ]τα Wilcken; ῥᾷσ]τα Kalinka.

429–30 ἑκ[ατέρας τῶν ἑ|ταιρει]ῶν Bartoletti; ἑκ[ατέρου τῶν| μερ]ῶν Grenfell and Hunt.

432 The papyrus reads]ροκλειδην.

84

XVII.1   In Thebes the best and most notable of the citizens, as I have already said, were in dispute with each other about politics.   One faction was led by Ismenias, Antitheus and Androcleidas, the other by Leontiades, Asias, and Coeratadas.   Leontiades' party supported the Spartans; Ismenias' party was accused of supporting the Athenians, arising from their support for the demos when it was in exile.   However, they were not concerned for the Athenians, but ... when ... they chose rather ... being ready to do evil.   XVII.2 Since this was the position in Thebes and both parties were influential, many came forward from the cities in Boeotia and joined one or other of the factions.   At that time and even a little earlier the party of Ismenias and Androcleidas was dominant among the Thebans

[παρὰ] τῇ βο[υλ]ῇ τῶν Βοιωτῶν, ἔμπρ[οσθεν δὲ] προ- |
[εῖχο]ν οἱ π[ε]ρὶ τὸν Ἀστίαν καὶ Λεοντ[ιάδην, χρόνον | δέ
τι]να συχνὸν καὶ τὴν πόλιν διὰ κ[ράτους εἶ]χον. | 3 ¹⁵[ὅτ]ε
γὰρ πολεμοῦντες οἱ Λακεδαιμ[όνιοι τοῖς] Ἀ[θην]αίοις ἐν
Δεκελείᾳ διέτριβον καὶ σύσ[τη]μ[α] τ[ῶ]ν α[ὑ]τῶν συμμάχων πολὺ συνεῖχον, οὗτοι μ[ᾶ]λλον ἐδυνάστευον τῶν
ἑτέρων, ἅμα μὲν τῷ πλ[η]σίον εἶναι τοὺς Λακε[δ]αιμον[ί-]
ους, ἅμα δὲ τῷ πολλὰ [τὴ]ν | ²⁰πόλιν εὐεργετε[ῖ]σθαι δι' 440
αὐτῶν. ἐπ[έδοσαν δὲ οἱ] Θηβαῖοι πολὺ πρὸς εὐδαιμονίαν
ὁλόκλ[ηρον . . . . ε]ὐθέως ὡς ὁ πόλεμος τοῖς Ἀθηναίοις
[συνέστη καὶ] τοῖς Λακεδαιμονίοις· ἀρξαμένων γὰρ ἀ-
[ταίρ]ειν τῶν Ἀθηναίων τῇ Βοιωτίᾳ συνῳκίσθησαν [εἰ]ς
αὐ|²⁵τὰς οἵ τ' ἐξ Ἐρυθρῶν καὶ Σκαφῶν καὶ Σκώλου κα[ὶ
Αὐ]λίδος καὶ Σχοίνου καὶ Ποτνιῶν καὶ πολλῶν ἑτέρων
τοιούτων χωρίων, ἃ τεῖχος οὐκ ἔχοντα διπλασίας ἐποίησεν
τὰς Θήβας. 4 οὐ μὴν ἀλλὰ πολύ γε βέλτιον ἔτι τὴν πόλιν
πρᾶξαι συνέπεσεν, ὡς τὴν Δεκέλειαν ἐπετεί|³⁰χισαν τοῖς
Ἀθηναίοις μετὰ τῶν Λακεδ[αι]μ[ονί]ων· τά τε γὰρ ἀνδρά- 450
ποδα καὶ τὰ λοιπὰ πάντ[α ⟨τὰ⟩ κατὰ τὸ]ν πόλεμον ἁλι-
σκόμενα μικροῦ τιν[ος ἀργυρίο]υ παρελάμβανον, καὶ τὴν
ἐκ τῆς Ἀττικῆ[ς κ]ατα[σ]κευὴν ἅτε πρόσχωροι κατοικοῦν-
τες ἅπασαν μετεκόμι|³⁵σαν ὡς αὐτούς, ἀπὸ τῶν ξύλων καὶ
τοῦ κεράμου τοῦ τῶν οἰκιῶν ἀρξάμενοι. 5 τότε δὲ τῶν Ἀθηναίων ἡ χώρα πολυτελέστατα τῆς Ἑλλάδος κατεσκεύ-
αστο· ἐπεπόνθει γὰρ μικρὰ κακῶς ἐν ταῖς ἐμβολαῖς ταῖς
ἔμπροσθεν ὑπὸ τῶν Λακεδαιμονίων, ὑπὸ δὲ τῶν | ⁴⁰Ἀθη-
ναίων οὕτως ἐξήσκητο καὶ διεπεπόνητο κα|[θ' ὑπε]ρβο-·

---

435 κ[ράτους Crönert; π[είθους Richards: the
  downstroke on the very edge of the preserved
  portion could be κ, π, γ, μ, or ν.
443–4 ἀν[ταίρ]ειν Kalinka; ἀπ[ειλ]εῖν Grenfell
  and Hunt.

themselves and in the council of the Boeotians, but previously the party of Asias and Leontiades had control in the city for some length of time.

XVII.3   When the Spartans were at Deceleia during the war against the Athenians, and gathered their allies there *en masse*, this party was more dominant than the other, partly because the Spartans were nearby, partly because the city was profiting considerably on their account. The Thebans had advanced greatly towards complete prosperity as soon as the war between Athens and Sparta began. For when the Athenians began to move against Boeotia, those who lived in Erythrae, Scaphae, Scolus, Aulis, Schoenus, Potniae and many other such places which had no walls, were gathered into Thebes and doubled its size.   XVII.4   And indeed it happened that the city fared even better when, with the Spartans, they fortified Deceleia against the Athenians. For they bought up the slaves and the rest of the stuff captured in the war for a small price, and, since they lived in the neighbouring areas, they carried home all the equipment from Attica, starting with the timber and the tiles of the houses.

XVII.5   At that time the Athenians' territory was the most lavishly equipped part of Greece, for it had suffered only slight damage from the Spartans in the previous attacks and it had been adorned and crafted so elegantly

λήν, ὥ[στε ....]δὲν παρ' αὐτοῖς ἐπα[. | ...., ο]ἰκή- 460
σει[ς δὲ .... ᾠ]κοδομημένας ἢ πα[ρὰ το]ῖς ἄλλοις
[............][.. τοσ] γὰρ αὐτῶν ἃ πα[ρὰ τῶ]ν Ἑλ-
λήν[ων πολεμοῦντε]ς ἐλάμβανον εἰς τοὺ[ς | ⁵ἰδίο]υς ἀγροὺς
ἀ[νήγαγε. τὰ μὲν ο]ὖν πράγματα τὰ κατ[ὰ τὰ]ς Θήβας
καὶ τ[ὴν Βοιωτίαν εἶχεν] οὕτως.

XVIII (XIII) Οἱ δὲ περὶ τὸν Ἀ[ν]δροκλείδαν κα[ὶ τὸν
Ἰσμηνίαν ἐ]σπούδαζον ἐκπολεμῶσαι τὸ ἔθνος [πρὸς τοὺς
Λακεδα]ιμονίους, βουλόμενοι μὲν καταλῦσαι τ[ὴν ἀρχὴν
αὐτῶ]ν ἵνα μὴ διαφθαρῶσιν | ¹⁰ὑπ' ἐκείνων διὰ [τοὺς
λακων]ίζοντας, οἰόμενοι δὲ ῥᾳδίως τοῦτο πρ[άξειν ὑπο- 470
λα]μβάνοντες βασιλ[έ]α χρήματα π[α]ρέξε[ιν, ὅπερ ὁ π]αρὰ
τοῦ βαρβάρου π[ε]μφθεὶς ἐπηγγέλλετο, ⟨τοὺς δὲ⟩ [Κοριν-
θίου]ς καὶ τοὺς Ἀργείου[ς] καὶ τοὺς Ἀ[θη]ναίους μεθέ-
[ξειν τοῦ] πολέμου· τούτους γὰρ | ¹⁵ἐχθροὺς τοῖς Λακε-

---

460 ὥ[στε χώρας ἦν οὐ]δὲν παρ' αὐτοῖς
  ἐπά[ρατον Bury; ὥ[στε εἶναι μη]δὲν παρ'
  αὐτοῖς ἐπα[κτόν Fuhr (same in Grenfell and
  Hunt², with ὑπάρχειν instead of εἶναι, to fill
  up space); ὥ[στε φαῦλον ἦν οὐ]δὲν παρ'
  αὐτοῖς ἐπα[ύλιον Keil; ὥ[στε εὐτελὲς
  μη]δὲν παρ' αὐτοις ἐπα[ύλιον Lipsius.
  ο]ἰκήσει[ς δὲ καὶ κάλλιον ᾠ]κοδομημένας
  Bury; λαμπρότερον Fuhr; εὐπρεπέστερον
  Gigante.
462 After a lost portion there are the crossed-out
  letters τοσ: possibly part of a corrected
  dittography, for example εκαστοσστος (Keil).
472 ⟨τοὺς δὲ⟩[Κορινθίου]ς Grenfell and Hunt;
  [ἔτι δ'ἴσω]ς Kalinka.

by the Athenians that ... with them ... dwellings ... having been built or with others ... of them what they took when fighting from the Greeks they led to their own fields. Such was the situation in Thebes and in Boeotia.

XVIII.1 The party of Androcleidas and Ismenias hastened to engage the people in war against the Spartans, wanting to overthrow their empire, so that they would not be swept aside by the Spartans because of the pro−Spartan party. They thought that they would achieve this easily, supposing that the King would provide the money which the envoy from Persia had promised, and that the Corinthians, Argives and Athenians would share in the war, since, being enemies

δαιμ[ονίοις ὄ]ντας αὐτοῖς συμπαρ⟨α⟩[σκ]ευάσε⟨ιν⟩ τοὺς πολίτας. 2 [δι]ανοηθέντες δὲ ταῦτα περὶ τῶν πραγμάτων ἐνόμιζον ἀπὸ μὲν τοῦ φανεροῦ χαλεπῶς ἔχειν ἐπιτίθεσθαι τούτοις· οὐδέποτε γὰρ οὔτε Θηβαίους οὔτε τοὺς ἄλλους Βοιωτοὺς πεισθή|²⁰σεσθαι πολεμεῖν Λακεδαιμονίοις ἄρχουσι τῆς Ἑλλάδος· ἐπιχειροῦντες [δ]ὲ διὰ ταύτης τῆς 480 ἀπάτης προάγειν εἰς τὸν πόλεμον αὐτούς, ἀνέπεισαν ἄνδρας τινὰς Φωκέων ἐμβαλεῖν εἰς τὴν Λοκρῶν τῶν Ἑσπερίων καλουμένων, οἷς ἐγένετο τῆς ἔχθρας αἰτία τοιαύτη. |
3 ²⁵ἔστι τοῖς ἔθνεσιν τούτοις ἀμφισβητήσιμος χώρα περὶ τὸν Παρνασσόν, περ[ὶ] ἧς καὶ πρότερόν ποτε πεπολεμήκασιν, ἣν πολλάκις ἐπινέμουσιν ἑκάτεροι τῶν τε Φωκέων καὶ τῶν Λοκρῶν, ὁπότεροι δ' ἂν τύχωσιν αἰσθόμενοί ποτε ⟨τοὺς⟩ ἑτέρους συλλεγέντες πολλοὶ διαρπάζουσι | ³⁰τὰ πρόβατα. πρότερον μὲν οὖν πολλῶν τοιούτων ἀφ' ἑκατέρων γιγνομένων ἀεὶ μετὰ δίκης τὰ πολλὰ καὶ λόγων 490 διελύοντο πρὸς ἀλλήλους, τότε δὲ τῶν Λοκρῶν ἀνθαρπασάντων ἀνθ' ὧν ἀπέβαλον προβάτων εὐθὺς οἱ Φωκε[ῖ]ς, παροξυνόντων αὐτοὺς ἐκείνων τῶν | ³⁵ἀνδρῶν ο[ὓς οἱ] περὶ τὸν Ἀνδροκλείδαν καὶ τὸν Ἰσμηνίαν παρεσκεύασαν, εἰς τὴν Λοκρίδα μετὰ τῶν ὅπλων ἐνέβαλον. 4 οἱ δὲ Λοκροὶ δῃουμένης τῆς χώρας πέμψαντες πρέσβεις εἰς Βοιωτοὺς κατηγορίαν ἐπο[ιο]ῦντο τῶν Φ[ω]κέων, καὶ βοηθεῖν ἐκείνους αὐτοῖς | ⁴⁰[ἠξίο]υν· διάκειν[τ]αι δὲ πρὸς αὐτοὺς ἀεί ποτε φιλίως. || [ἁρπ]άσαντες δὲ τὸν καιρὸν ἀσμ[ένως μάλα οἱ περὶ τὸν Ἰσ]μηνίαν καὶ τὸν Ἀνδροκλε[ίδαν ἔπει- 500 σαν τοὺς Βοι]ωτοὺς βοηθεῖν τοῖς Λοκροῖς. Φω[κεῖς δέ,

---

475 The papyrus reading συνπαρε[..]ευασε does not yield a grammatical sentence: συμπαρ<α>[σκ]ευάσε<ιν> Grenfell and Hunt; συνπαρε[σκ]εύασε τὸ <ἰσονομεῖσθαι το>ὺς Kalinka.

of the Spartans, they would secure the support of their citizens.

XVIII.2 This was their analysis of the situation; but they thought that it would be difficult to attack them openly, since neither the Thebans nor the Boeotians would ever be persuaded to make war on the Spartans, who were supreme in Greece. This was the trick they used to lead them into war: they persuaded certain men among the Phocians to launch an attack on the territory of the Western Locrians.

Enmity between them arose from the following cause: XVIII.3 these peoples have a disputed area near Mount Parnassus, over which they had previously fought, which both Phocians and Locrians often encroached on for grazing. Whichever side it was which noticed the other side doing this, collected together a large force and made a sheep raid. Many such incidents had arisen previously from both sides, but the sides were reconciled to each other on those occasions for the most part through arbitration and discussions with each other; but on this particular occasion the Locrians seized in return an equivalent number of sheep for the ones they had lost, and straightaway the Phocians, urged on by those men whom the party of Androcleidas and Ismenias had put up to it, invaded Locris under arms.

XVIII.4 With their territory being ravaged, the Locrians, having sent ambassadors to the Boeotians, made accusations against the Phocians and demanded that the Boeotians help them. These states had always enjoyed good relations. The party of Ismenias and Androcleidas gladly seized their opportunity and persuaded the Boeotians to help the Locrians. But the Phocians, when

ἀγγελθέντ]ων αὐτοῖς τῶν ἐκ τῶν Θηβῶν, τ[ότε μὲν ἐκ τῆς
Λοκρίδος | ⁵π]άλιν ἀνεχώρησαν, πρέσβεις δ[ὲ] πα[ραχρῆμα
πέμψαν]τες πρὸς Λακεδαιμονίους ἠξίουν ἐκ[είνους ἀπει-]
πεῖν Βοιωτοῖς εἰς τὴν αὐτῶν βαδίζ[ειν. οἱ δὲ καίπερ] λέ-
γειν αὐτοὺς νομίσαντες ἄπιστα, [πέμψαντες ὅμως] οὐκ εἴων
τοὺς Βοιωτοὺς πόλεμον ἐκ[φέρειν πρὸς τοὺς] | ¹⁰Φωκέας,
ἀλλ᾽ εἴ τι ἀδικεῖσθαι νομίζουσ[ι δίκην λαμ]βάνειν παρ᾽
αὐτῶν ἐν τοῖς συμμάχοις [ἐκέλευον. οἱ δέ, πα]ροξυνόντων
αὐτοὺς τῶν καὶ τὴν ἀπ[άτην καὶ τὰ πρά]γματα ταῦτα 510
συστησάντων, τοὺς μὲν [πρέσβεις τοὺς] τῶν Λακεδαι-
μονίων ἀπράκτους ἀπέστε[ιλαν, αὐτοὶ δὲ] | ¹⁵τὰ ὅπλα
λαβόντες ἐβάδ[ι]ζον ἐπὶ τοὺς Φωκέ[ας. 5 ἐμβα]λόν-
τες δὲ διὰ ταχέων εἰς τὴν Φωκίδα καὶ [πορθ]ή-
σαντες τήν τε τῶν Παραποταμίων χώραν καὶ Δαυλίων
καὶ Φανοτέων ἐπεχείρησαν ταῖς πόλεσι προσβάλλειν· καὶ
Δαυλίᾳ μὲν προσελθόντες ἀπεχώρησαν αὖθις | ²⁰οὐδὲν
ποιήσαντες, ἀλλὰ καὶ πληγὰς ὀλίγας λαβόντες, Φανοτέων δὲ τὸ προάστιον κατὰ κράτος εἷλον. διαπραξάμενοι
δὲ ταῦτα προῆλθον εἰς τὴν Φωκίδα, καταδραμόντες δὲ 520
μέρος τι τοῦ πεδίου ⟨τοῦ⟩ περὶ τὴν Ἐλάτειαν καὶ τοὺς
Πεδιέας καὶ τοὺς ταύτῃ κατοικοῦν|²⁵τας ἀπῄεσαν. ποι-
ουμένων δὲ τὴν ἀποχώρησιν αὐτῶν {προσ} παρ᾽ Ὑ⟨άμ⟩πο-
λιν ἔδοξεν αὐτοῖς ἀποπειρᾶσθαι τῆς πόλεως· ἔστι δὲ τὸ

---

503 πα[ραχρῆμα Fuhr; πα[ραυτίκα Boissevain;
τ]ι̣ν̣[ας προσπέμψαν]τες Richards. The traces
of the dotted letters are almost non−existent.
509 [ἐκέλευον. οἱ δέ, πα] Grenfell and Hunt;
Βοιωτοὶ δὲ Fuhr.
510 ταρά]γματα? Wilcken.
523 {πρὸς} παρ᾽ Ὑ⟨άμ⟩ πολιν Blass and
Wilamowitz; παρ᾽ Ὕην πόλιν Kalinka; παρ᾽
Ὕαν πόλιν Gigante. The papyrus reads
προσπαρυηνπολιν.

news reached them of events at Thebes, retreated from Locris, and sending envoys at once to the Spartans they asked them to forbid the Boeotians from entering their territory. The Spartans, although they thought the story was unworthy of belief, sent envoys and told the Boeotians not to make war on the Phocians, but if they thought that they were wronged in any way, they ordered them to obtain justice from them in a meeting of their allies. With the people who had set up the whole deceitful business urging them on, the Boeotians sent away the envoys of the Spartans with nothing achieved, then themselves took up arms and marched against the Phocians.

XVIII.5 Having invaded Phocis swiftly and ravaged the land of the Parapotamians, Daulians and Phanotians, they attempted to assault the cities. After attacking Daulis they retreated with nothing achieved — in fact they sustained some losses; they captured by force the suburb of Phanotis. After achieving this they advanced into Phocis and, having overrun part of the plain round Elatea and Pedieis and those living in that region, they went away. While they were making this retreat in the neighbourhood of Hyampolis they decided to make an attempt on the town. This place is reasonably strong.

χωρίον ἐπ⟨ι⟩εικῶς ἰσχυρόν· προσβαλόντες δὲ τοῖς τείχεσι καὶ προθυμίας οὐδὲν ἐλλιπόντες ἄλλο μὲν οὐδὲν ἔπραξαν, ἀποβαλόντες δὲ | ³⁰τῶν στρατιωτῶν ὡς ὀγδοήκοντα πάλιν ἀνεχώρησαν. Βοιωτοὶ μὲν ο[ὖ]ν τοσαῦτα κακὰ ποιήσαντες [τ]οὺς Φωκέ[α]ς ἀπῆλθον εἰς τὴν ἑαυτῶν.

XIX (XIV) Κόνων δέ, παρειληφότος ἤδη Χειρικρά- 530 τους τὰς ναῦς τὰς τῶν Λακεδαιμονίων καὶ τῶν συμμάχων, ὃς ἀφίκετο ναύαρχος διά|³⁵δοχος τῷ Πόλλιδι, συμπληρώσας εἴκοσι τῶν τριήρων ἀναγόμενος ἐκ τῆς Ῥόδου κατέπλευσεν εἰς Καῦνον· βουλόμενος δὲ συμμεῖξαι τῷ Φαρναβάζῳ κα[ὶ] τῷ Τιθραύστῃ καὶ χρήματα λαβεῖν ἀνέβαινεν ἐκ τῆς Καύνου πρὸς αὐτούς. **2** ἐτύγχανε δὲ τοῖς στρατιώ‖ταις κατὰ τοῦτον τὸν χρόνον προσοφειλόμενος μισθὸς πολλῶν μηνῶν· ἐμισθοδοτ[οῦ]ντο γὰρ ὑπὸ τῶν στρατηγῶν κακῶς, ὃ ποιεῖν ἔθ[ος] ἐστὶν ἀεὶ τοῖς πολεμοῦσι⟨ν⟩ ὑπὲρ βασιλέως, ἐπε[ὶ ⟨καὶ⟩ κα]τὰ τὸν | ⁵Δεκε- 540 λεικὸν πόλεμον, ὁπότε σύμμ[αχοι] Λακεδαιμονίοι⟨ς⟩ ἦσαν, κομιδῇ φαύλως καὶ γλίσχ[ρω]ς παρείχοντο χρήματα, καὶ πολλάκις ἂν κατ[ε]λύθησαν αἱ τῶν συμμάχων τρ[ι]ήρεις εἰ μὴ διὰ τὴν Κύρου προθυμίαν. τούτων δὲ βασιλεὺς αἴτιός ἐστι⟨ν⟩, ὃς | ¹⁰ἐπειδὰν ἐνστήσηται πόλεμον καταπέμψας κατ' ἀρχὰς ὀλίγα χρήματα τοῖς ἄρχουσιν ὀλιγωρεῖ τὸν ἐπίλοιπον χρόνον, οἱ δὲ τοῖς πράγμασιν ἐφεστῶτες οὐκ ἔχοντες ἀναλίσκειν ἐκ τῶν ἰδίων πε[ριορῶ]σιν ἐνίοτε καταλυομέν[α]ς τὰς αὐτῶν | ¹⁵[δυνάμ]εις. **3** ταῦτα μὲν οὖν οὕτως συμβαίνειν εἴωθε· Τιθραύστης δέ, παρα- 550 γενομένου τοῦ Κόνωνος ὡς αὐτὸν καὶ λέγοντος ὅτι κινδυνεύσει συντριβῆναι τὰ πράγματα διὰ χρημάτων ἔνδειαν,

---

541 Λακεδαιμονιοι< ς> Wilamowitz.
551 The αυ of αὐτὸν is a correction written over something else.

After attacking the walls and lacking nothing in enthusiasm, all they achieved was the loss of about eighty men: and they retreated again. Having done that much damage to the Phocians, the Boeotians returned to their own country.

XIX.1 Now that Cheiricrates had arrived as admiral in succession to Pollis and had already taken over command of the ships of the Spartans and their allies, Conon manned twenty of the triremes and set out from Rhodes and sailed to Caunus. Wishing to communicate with Pharnabazus and Tithraustes and to get money, he went up from Caunus to them. XIX.2 It happened that at this time the soldiers were owed many months pay. For they were badly paid by the generals — which is normal practice for those fighting for the King, as in the Decelean War when they were allies of the Spartans, they provided the money on an altogether mean and niggardly scale, and the triremes of their allies would often have been disbanded had it not been for the energy of Cyrus. The responsibility for this lies with the King who, whenever it is decided to make war, sends a small sum of money at the beginning to those in charge and takes no account of the future. And those in charge of affairs, not having the means to pay from their private fortunes, sometimes permit the disbandment of their forces.

XIX.3 This is what usually happens. But when Conon arrived in his presence and said that there was a risk of everything falling apart for lack of money, and that it

οἷς τοὺς ὑπὲρ βασιλέως πολεμοῦντας οὐκ εὐλό|[20]γως ἔχειν ἀπαγορεύ[ε]ιν, ἀποστέλλει τινὰς τῶν μεθ' αὑτοῦ βαρβάρων ἵνα μισθὸν δῶσι τοῖς στρατιώταις, ἔχοντας ἀργυρίου τάλαντα διακόσια καὶ εἴκοσι⟨ν⟩· ἐλήφθη δὲ τοῦτο ⟨τὸ⟩ ἀργύριον ἐκ τῆς οὐσίας τῆς Τισσαφέρνους. Τιθραύστης μὲν οὖν ἔτι περιμεί|[25]νας ὀλίγον χρόνον ἐν ταῖς Σάρδεσιν ἀνέβαινεν ὡς βασιλέα, καταστήσας στρατηγοὺς ἐπὶ τῶν πραγμάτων Ἀριαῖον καὶ Πασιφέρνη καὶ παραδοὺς αὐτοῖς εἰς τὸν πόλεμον τὸ καταλειφθὲν ἀργύριον καὶ χρυσίον, ὅ φασι φανῆναι περὶ ἑπτακόσια τάλαντα.

XX (XV) Τῶν | [30]δὲ Κυπρίων οἱ μετὰ τοῦ Κόνωνος καταπλεύσαντες εἰς τὴν Καῦνον, ἀναπεισθέντες οὕτω τινῶν διαβαλλόντων, ὡς αὐτοῖς μὲν οὐ μέλλουσιν ἀποδιδόναι τὸν μισθὸν τὸν ὀφειλόμενον, παρασκευάζονται δὲ διαλύσ[ει]ς μόνον τα[ῖ]ς ὑπηρεσίαις | [35]καὶ τοῖς ἐπιβάταις, χαλεπῶς ἔφερον, καὶ συνελθόντες εἰς ἐκκλησίαν εἵλοντο στρα[τ]ηγὸν αὑτῶν ἄνδρα Καρπασέα τὸ γέ[ν]ος, καὶ το[ύτ]ῳ φυλακὴν ἔδοσαν τοῦ σώματος δύο σ[τρατι]ώτας ἀφ' ἑκάστης ‖ [τάξεως . . . .]ιπ[. . . . .
. . .]ν | [. . . . .]κ α . . [. .]των[. . . . .|
. . . .] τὸν Κόνωνα [. . . . . | . . . .
. . . .]ως ἐτύγχανε . [. . . . .]υσ[. . . . . . |⁵. . . .
.]αραιει κατελ[θόντος τοῦ Κό]νωνος . [. . | . . . . διελέ]γετο περὶ τῶ[ν πραγμάτ]ων. **2** Κόνων δὲ ω[. | . . . . α]ὑτῶν

---

556 εἴκοσι⟨ν⟩ Keil.
576 τῷ[ν πραγμάτ]ων Bartoletti; τῶ[ν χρέ]ων Kalinka; τῶ[ν ἔργ]ων Gigante. δὲ ᾡ[Bartoletti; δὲ ᾠ[Grenfell and Hunt; the traces could be of either letter.

was not right that those fighting on behalf of the King should fail for this reason, Tithraustes despatched some of the barbarians with him to give pay to the soldiers, and they had two hundred and twenty talents of silver. This money was taken from the resources of Tissaphernes. Tithraustes, after waiting a short time in Sardis, went inland to the King, having appointed Ariaeus and Pasiphernes as generals in charge of affairs, and having given them for the purposes of the war the silver and gold left behind, which (they say) was about seven hundred talents.

XX.1 Those of the Cypriots in Conon's forces sailed to Caunus and were persuaded, by some who spread false rumours, that they were not intending to give them the pay that was owing but were preparing discharges only for crews and marines. They were angry at this and got up a meeting and chose as their general a man of Carpasian race, and gave him as a bodyguard two soldiers from each company ... Conon ... as it happened ... when Conon was coming down ... negotiated about the matters in hand. XX.2 Conon ... did not allow

τ[οὺς . . . . . ο]υς οὐκ εἴα πιστεύειν | [. . . . .]
εκλ[.] . [. . . . . . . τῶν] Ἑλλήνων, ἀλ[λ]ὰ πάν|[τας ἔφη
τὸν μισθὸν ἀπὸ τῆς ἴση]ς κομιεῖσθαι, ταύτην | ¹⁰[δὲ τὴν
ἀπόκρισιν ποιησάμενος] ἔφασκεν βούλεσθαι [δι]α[δηλῶ- 580
σαι καὶ τοῖς ἄλλ]οις· ὁ δὲ στρατηγὸς ὁ τῶν [Κ]υπρ[ίων
ὁ Καρπα]σε[ὺς αὐτῷ] πρὸς τὸ πλῆθος τὸ τῶν στρατιω[τῶν
ἠ]κολο[ύθει. 3 ἐκ]ειν[ο]υ δὲ συνεξορμήσαντ[ο]ς, ἐπε[ιδὴ
πορ]ευόμεν[οι κα]τὰ τὰς πύλας ἦσαν, ὁ μὲν | ¹⁵Κόνων
[ὥσπερ] ἔτυχεν ἡγ[ού]μενος ἐξεληλύθει πρότερος ἐκ τ[οῦ
τείχους, τοῦ δὲ ἀ[νθ]ρώπου τοῦ Καρπασέως, ὡς ἦν ἐξι[ὼ]ν
κατὰ τὰς πύλας, ἐπιλαμβάνονται τῶν Μεσσηνίω[ν] τινὲς
τῶν τῷ Κόνωνι παρακολουθεῖν εἰωθότων, [οὐ] μετὰ τῆς
ἐκείνου γν[ώ]μης, ἐπιθυμοῦντες ἐν | ²⁰τῇ πόλε[ι] κατασχεῖν
αὐτόν, ὅπ[ως] ἂν ὧν ἐξήμαρτεν δῷ δίκ[η]ν. οἱ δὲ συν- 590
ακολουθο[ῦντ]ες τῶν Κυπρίων ἀντελαμ[β]άν[ο]ντο τ[οῦ
Καρπασέ]ως καὶ διεκώλυον τοὺς Μεσση[νιους] ἄγει[ν
αὐτόν, α]ἰσθανόμενον δὲ καὶ τὸ τῶν ἐξ[ω Κυπρ]ίων [πλῆ-
θος ἐπ]εβοήθει τῷ στρατηγῷ. ὁ·[δ]ὲ | ²⁵Κόνων [. . . . .]
πε[. . . . .] τοὺ[ς] ἀνθρώπους εἰσπηδήσας [. . . . .
. . . .]υσεν [ε]ἰς τὴν πόλιν· οἱ δὲ Κύπριοι τ[οὺς
Μεσσηνίους τοὺ]ς ἁψαμένους τοῦ Κα[ρ]πασέω[ς βά]λ-
λ[οντες ἀπέκρο]υσαν, αὐτοὶ δὲ πεπεισμ[έ]νοι πάντα π[αρὰ
τὸ προσῆκον τ]ὸν Κόνωνα παρε|³⁰σκευάσθαι περ[ὶ τὴν τοῦ
μισθοῦ] διάδοσιν ε[ἰσέ]β[αι]νον ε[ἰ]ς τὰς τρ[ιήρ]εις ἐπ[ὶ 600

577−8   οὐδένα πλεον]εκτ[ή]σ[ειν Grenfell and Hunt;
        ]εκλ[Bartoletti.
593   ἐξ[ω Κυπρ]ίων Lipsius; ἐξ[ακοσ]ίων Grenfell and
        Hunt; [πλῆθος ἐπ]εβοήθει Keil;
        [σύνταγμα]ἐβοήθει Grenfell and Hart.
595−6   ἀναβαίνειν ἐκέλε]υσεν Grenfell and Hunt²;
        [πάλιν ἔξωθεν ἀπέκρο]υσεν Boissevain;
        [συνεισπίπτειν ἐκώλ]υσεν Lipsius.
598−9   π[αρὰ τὸ προσῆκον τ]ὸν Grenfell and Hunt²;
        π[αρὰ τὰς συνθήκας τ]ὸν Lipsius.

them to believe ... of the Greeks, but said that all would receive their pay equally. Having made this reply he asserted that he wanted to explain this to the others. The general of the Cypriots, the Carpasian, followed him towards the mass of the soldiers. XX.3 They went out together and when they were passing the gates, Conon, who happened to be leading, had come out of the wall first. But some Messenians who usually accompanied Conon, seized the Carpasian man, without Conon's approval, as he was in the gateway on his way out, wishing to keep him in the city so that he would be punished for his crimes.

Those of the Cypriots who were accompanying him seized hold of the Carpasian and prevented the Messenians leading him off, and the crowd of Cypriots outside the gate, seeing what was happening, came up to the help of the general. But Conon ... having rushed into the midst of the men ... into the city. The Cypriots, having attacked the Messenians who had seized the Carpasian, drove them off, and since they were sure that Conon had made all the arrangements for the distribution of the pay in an unjust way, they embarked on the triremes — and this was the reason, (as some

ταύταις τ]αῖς πράξεσιν, ὥς γέ τινες ἔλεγον, [μ]έλλον[τες τοὺς ἐκ] τῆς Ῥόδου πορ[α]λιβόν[τε]ς εἰς Κύπρον πλε[ῖν, 4......]εύσαντες δὲ τῆς α|.αι[..]ιιοιον καὶ παραχ[αλέσαν]τες τοὺς βουλομέ|³⁵[νους τῶν Κ]υπρίων, βαδι[......] πρὸς τὴν ἀκρόπο|[λιν, ἵνα τὴ]ν ἀρχὴν τ[..... .....] καταλύσωσι⟨ν⟩ ὡς | [αἰτίου μό]νου πάν[των αὐτοῖς τῶ]ν κακῶν, ὁμοί|[ως δὲ ......π]οιησ[.......... ...]ν αὐτοῖς εἰσ|[............]εσια[......... ....] τῶν λόγων | ⁴⁰[................... ......]·[..] τὴν || πόλιν τα[................... 610 ...ἀ]ποπλεύσαν|τες ἀπὸ τῆς·[................] ·[...]μενοι | χρήσασθαι τοῖς αὐτ[.......... τῶν] τριήρων. 5 Κό|νων δὲ κατηγμέ[νων αὐτῶν προσ]ελθὼν πρὸς | ⁵Λεώνυμον τὸν τ[ῶν πεζῶν ὕπαρχον εἶ]π[ε]ν αὐτῷ ὅτι μόνος δύναται τ[ὰ πράγματα σῶσαι] τ[ὰ βα]σιλέως· εἰ γὰρ αὐτῷ βούλεται δ[οῦναι τούς τε φρο]υροὺς τοὺς [Ἕλ]ληνας,

---

603 ἀποπλ]εύσαντες Grenfell and Hunt, who expressed doubts about its use simply with a genitive; κυρι]εύσαντες Boissevain.
α[.αψ[..]νιοιου: ἐπιπλ]εύσαντες δὲ τῇ Σαλ[λ]αμ[εῖ]νι ὅπου Kalinka.
605 βαδί[ζουσιν] Grenfell and Hunt; βαδι[εῖσθαι] ? Bartoletti.
605-6 τ[οῦ Κόνωνος] Wilamowitz.
612 β[ουλό]μενοι Grenfell and Hunt; οὐ] δ[υνά]μενοι ? Bartoletti. αὐτ[όθεν ἱστίοις τῶν] Grenfell and Hunt; αὐτ[όθι σκεύεσι τῶν] Lipsius; αὐτ[όθεν σιτίοις τῶν] Gigante.
613 αὐτῶν προσ[ελθὼν Bartoletti; Κυπρίων] ἐλθὼν Grenfell and Hunt.
614 ὕπαρχον Keil; ἄρχοντα Wilamowitz.
616 δ[οῦναι τούς τε Bartoletti; δ[ιδόναι τοὺς Genfell and Hunt.

said): they proposed to take the people from Rhodes and sail to Cyprus ...   XX.4   ... having sailed away ... and having called together those of the Cypriots who wanted, going towards the acropolis so that they might overthrow the power of ... as being the cause of all their troubles, similarly ... for them ... of the speeches ... the city ... having sailed away from the ... to use the ... of the triremes.

XX.5   After they had put to sea, Conon came to Leonymus, the commander of the infantry, and said to him that he was the only one who could save the King's campaign. For if he would give him the Greek garrison, which

οἳ τὴν Καῦνον [φρουροῦσι, καὶ] τῶν Καρῶν ὡς πλείστους,
παύσει[ν τὴν ἐν τῷ στ]ρατοπέδῳ τα|¹⁰ραχήν. κελεύσαντος
δ[ὲ τοῦ Λεωνύμ]ου λαμβάνειν ὁπόσους βούλεται στρατ[ι-
ώτας, ταύτ]ην μὲν τὴν ἡμέραν παρῆκεν, καὶ γὰρ ἦ[ν ἥλιος 620
ἤ]δη περὶ δυσμάς, εἰς δὲ τὴν ἐπιοῦσαν, πρὶν ἡμ[έραν
γ]ενέσθαι, λαβὼν παρὰ τοῦ Λεωνύμου τῶν τε [Καρῶν]
συχνοὺς καὶ τοὺς | ¹⁵Ἕλληνας ἅπαντας ἐξήγαγεν [αὐτο]ὺς
ἐκ τῆς πόλεως· ἔπειτα τοὺς μὲν [ἔξ]ωθεν αὐτοῦ τοῦ στρατοπέδου περιέστησεν, τοὺς [δὲ...].[.....]ν πρός τε
τὰς ναῦς κα[ὶ] τὸν αἰγιαλὸν [διετάξατο. τα]ῦτα δὲ ποιή-
σας καὶ κελεύσας κηρῦξαι τ[ὸν κήρυκα χω]ρεῖν ἕκαστον
τῶν στρα|²⁰τιωτῶν ἐπὶ τὴ[ν ἑαυτοῦ, συ]νέλαβε τῶν Κυ-
πρίων τόν τε Καρπασέ[α καὶ τῶν ἄλ]λων ἑξήκοντα, καὶ
τοὺς μὲν ἀπέκτειν[ε, τὸν δὲ στρα]τηγὸν ἀνεσταύρωσεν. 630
6 ἀκούσαντες δ[ὲ.........ο]ἱ καταλειφθέντες ἐν τῇ
Ῥόδῳ ⟨δι⟩ηγανάκτ[ουν, καὶ χαλεπ]ῶς ἐνεγκόντες τοὺς
μὲν | ²⁵ἄρχοντας τοὺς [ὑπὸ τοῦ Κόνω]νος καταστάντας
βάλλοντες ἐξήλασ[αν ἐκ τοῦ] στρατοπέδου, τὸν δὲ λιμένα
καταλιπόν[τες πολὺν] θόρυβον καὶ ταραχὴν παρ[έ]σχον

---

625 παρ]α[γαγὼ]ν Lipsius; ἐς φ]υ[λακὴ]ν
Castiglioni: nothing visible to P.McK.
corresponds to the letters α or υ.
626 [διετάξατο Lipsius; [προσήγαγε Grenfell and
Hunt; [κατέστησεν or [κατέταξεν Castiglioni.
627 χω]ρεῖν Bartoletti; βαί]νειν Wilamowitz.
628 τὴ[ν ἑαυτοῦ Wilamowitz; τη[ν σκηνὴν Bury.
631 δ[ὲ τὰ ἐκεῖθεν Keil; δ[ὲ τὰ γενόμενα
Grenfell and Hunt; δ[ὲ τὰ γεγονότα Fuhr; δ[ὲ
τὸ γεγονός Kalinka.
632 Ῥόδῳ <δι> ηγανάκτ[ουν Fuhr, to avoid the
hiatus: the papyrus reads Ῥόδῳ ἡγανάκτ[ουν.
χαλεπ]ῶς ἐνέγκοντες Bartoletti; βαρέ]ως
Grenfell and Hunt.

guarded Caunus, and as many Carians as possible, he would put a stop to the disturbance in the camp. Leonymus told him to take as many soldiers as he wanted. He let the day pass for the sun was already near to setting. But on the following day, before daybreak came, he took from Leonymus many of the Carians and all the Greeks, and led them from the city. Then he positioned some outside the camp, others ... near the ships and the seashore. After doing this and ordering the herald to announce that each man should go to his post, he arrested the Carpasian and sixty of the other Cypriots; he killed them and crucified their general. XX.6 Having heard ... those left behind in Rhodes were angry and indignant, and they attacked the commanders appointed by Conon and drove them out of the camp, and leaving the harbour they caused much disturbance and commotion among the Rhodians.

τοῖς Ῥοδ[ίοις· ὁ δὲ Κό]νων ἀφικόμενος ἐκ τῆς Καύνου
τούς τ[ε ἄρχοντ]ας αὐτῶν συλλαβὼν ἀπέκτει|³⁰νε καὶ τοῖς
ἄλλ[οις μισθὸ]ν διέδωκε. τὸ μὲν οὖν βασιλικὸν στρατό-
[πεδον οὕτ]ως εἰς μέγαν κίνδυνον προελθὸν διὰ Κόνων[α
καὶ] τὴν ἐκείνου προθυμίαν ἐπαύσατο τῆς ταραχῆ[ς.   640

XXI (XVI) Ἀ]γησίλαος δὲ παρα[π]ορευόμ[εν]ος εἰς
τὸν Ἑλλήσπ[ο]ντον ἅμα τῷ στρατ[ε]ύμα|³⁵τ[ι τῶν Λ]ακε-
δαιμονίων κ[α]ὶ τῶν συμμάχων ὅσον μὲν χ[ρόνο]ν ἐβά-
διζε διὰ τῆ[ς] Λυδίας [ο]ὐδὲν κακὸν ἐποί[ει τοὺς] ἐνοικοῦν-
τας, β[ουλ]όμενος ἐμμ[έν]ειν ταῖς σπον[δ]αῖ[ς τ]αῖς πρὸς
Τιθραύ[στ]ην γενομ[έναις·] ἐπειδὴ δὲ κα[τ]ῆρεν εἰς τὴν
χ[ώραν] τὴν Φαρν[αβά]ζου, προῆγε τὸ || στράτ[ε]υμα λεη-
λατῶν καὶ πορθῶν τὴ[ν γῆν. ἐπειδὴ] δὲ παραλλάξα[ς τ]ό
τε Θήβης πεδίον καὶ τ[ὸ Ἀπίας] καλούμενον ε[ἰσ]έβαλεν
εἰς τὴν Μυσία[ν, προσέκει]το τοῖς Μυσο[ῖ]ς κελ[εύω]ν   650
αὐτοὺς συστρ[ατεύειν με]|⁵τ' αὐτῶν· εἰσὶ γὰρ οἱ πολ-
[λ]οὶ [τ]ῶν Μυσῶν αὐ[τόνομοι καὶ] βασιλέως οὐχ ὑπα-
κούον[τ]ες. ὅσοι μὲν οὖν [τῶν Μυ]σῶν μετέχειν ᾑροῦντο
⁵ τῆς στρατείας, [οὐδὲν ἐ]ποίει κακὸν αὐτούς, τῶν δὲ λοιπῶν
ἐδήι[ου τὴν χώ]ραν. **2** ἐπειδὴ δὲ προϊὼν ἐγένετο κατὰ
μέσο[ν μάλι]|¹⁰στα τ[ὸ]ν Ὄλυμπον τὸν Μύσιον καλούμε-
ν[ον, ὁρῶν] χαλ[ε]πὴν καὶ στενὴν οὖσαν τὴν δίοδον [καὶ
βου]λόμ[ενος] ἀσφα[λῶ]ς πορευθῆναι δι' αὐτῆς, πέμ[ψας]
10 τινὰ[ς εἰ]ς τ[οὺς Μ]υσοὺς καὶ σπεισάμενος πρὸς α[ὐ]τοὺς
ἦ[γε τὸ] σ[τράτ]ευμα διὰ τῆς χώρας. παρέντ[ε]ς | ¹⁵δὲ   660
π. [. . . . . . . τῶν Π]ε[λ]οποννησίων καὶ τῶν συμ[μ]άχ[ων,

---

649 Ἀπίας] Wilamowitz.
650 προσέκει]το Lipsius; καὶ ἐνέκει]το Grenfell and Hunt
661 πο[λλοὺς Grenfell and Hunt; τὸ [πλῆθος Lipsius; πλ[είστους suggested by Bartoletti.

Arriving from Caunus, Conon captured their leaders and killed them, and gave pay to the others. And so the army of the King, having come into great danger, ceased from disorder on account of Conon and his energy.

XXI.1 Agesilaus, while advancing to the Hellespont with the army of the Spartans and their allies, as long as he was going through Lydia, caused no harm to the inhabitants, since he wished to abide by the truce agreed with Tithraustes. But when he swooped down into Pharnabazus' country he advanced with his army, plundering and ravaging the land. When he had crossed the plain of Thebe and the plain of Apia, as it is called, he invaded Mysia and put pressure on the Mysians, ordering them to campaign with him. For the majority of the Mysians are independent and not subjects of the King. He did no harm to those of the Mysians who chose to share in his expedition, but he ravaged the land of the rest.

XXI.2 When he came during his advance to the middle of the Mysian Olympus as it is called, seeing that the way through was difficult and narrow and wanting a safe passage through it, he sent some people to the Mysians and made terms with them and led his army through the region. Having let pass ... of the Peloponnesians

ἐπιθέμενοι τ]οῖς τελευταίοις αὐτῶν καταβάλλ[ουσι....
.... τ]ῶν στρατιωτῶν ἀτάκτων διὰ τὰς στ[ενοχωρίας
ὄντ]ων. Ἀγησίλαος δὲ καταζεύξας τ[ὸ στράτευμα τα]ύτην
τὴν ἡμέραν ἡσυχία[ν] | [20]ἦ[γε ποιῶν τὰ νο]μ[ιζ]όμενα
τοῖς ἀποθανοῦσι· διεφθάρη[σαν] δὲ περὶ πεντήκοντα τῶν
στρατιωτῶν· εἰς δὲ τ[ὴν] ἐπιοῦσαν καθίσας εἰς ἐνέδραν
πολλοὺς τῶν μ[ισθοφ]όρων τῶν Δερκυλιδείων καλουμένων
ἀνασ[τὰς πρ]οῆγε τὸ στράτευμα πάλιν. τῶν δὲ Μυσῶν |
[25]οἰηθ[έντες ἕ]καστοι διὰ τὴν πληγὴν τὴν τῇ προτερα[ίᾳ 670
γενο]μένην ἀπιέναι τὸν Ἀγησίλαον, ἐξελθόντ[ες ἐκ τ]ῶν
κωμῶν ἐδ.ωκον, ὡς ἐπιθησόμενοι τοῖς τ[ελευ]ταίοις τὸν
αὐτὸν τρόπον. οἱ δὲ τῶν Ἑλλήνων ἐ[νεδρεύ]οντες, ὡς ἦσαν
κατ' αὐτούς, ἐκπηδή|[30]σαντες ἐ[κ τ]ῆς ἐνέδρας εἰς χεῖρας
ᾖεσαν τοῖς πολεμίοις. τῶν δὲ Μυσῶν οἱ μὲν ἡγούμενοι καὶ
πρῶτοι διώκο[ν]τες ἐξαίφνης τοῖς Ἕλλησι συμμείξαντες
ἀποθ[ν]ήσκουσι⟨ν⟩, οἱ δὲ πολλοὶ κατιδόντες τοὺς πρώτους
α[ὐτῶ]ν ἐν πληγαῖς ὄντας ἔφευγον πρὸς τὰς κώ|[35]μας.
Ἀγ[ησίλ]αος δὲ προσαγγελθέντων αὐτῷ τούτων μετα[βαλό-
με]νος ἀπῆγε τὸ στράτευμα πάλιν τὴν αὐτὴν [ὁδόν, ἕ]ως 680
συνέμειξε τοῖς ἐν τα[ῖ]ς ἐνέδραις, καὶ κα[τεσκή]νωσεν εἰς
τὸ στρατόπεδον, ᾗ καὶ τῇ προτέρᾳ [κ]ατεστρατοπέδευ-
σ⟨ε⟩ν. **3** μετὰ δὲ ταῦτα τῶν ‖ μὲν Μυσῶν, ὧν ἦσαν [οἱ
ἀποθανόντες, ἕκαστοι κή]ρυκας πέμψαντες α[........
.... ἀνείλον]το τοὺς νεκροὺς ὑ[ποσπόνδους· ἀπέθα-
νον δὲ πλείους] ἢ τριάκοντα καὶ ἑ[κατόν· Ἀγησίλαος δὲ

664 ἰόντων] Cronert.
670–1 προτερα[ίᾳ γενο]μένην Fuhr; προτέρᾳ
 [γεγενη]μένην Grenfell and Hunt.
682 The papyrus reads [κ]ατεστρατοπέδευσαν;
 –σαν<το> (Fuhr) instead of –σ<ε>ν is a
 possibility.
684 ἀ[νοχὰς ἐποιοῦντο καὶ ἀνείλον]το Castiglioni.

and their allies, they attacked the rearguard and killed ... the soldiers being in disarray on account of the narrow place. Agesilaus encamped his army and passed the day quietly, performing the customary rituals for the dead. About fifty soldiers had been killed. On the following day he posted in an ambush many of the Dercylidean mercenaries, as they are called, and led his army forward again. Each of the Mysians thought that Agesilaus was going away on account of the loss received on the previous day, and they came out of their villages and began to pursue him with the intention of attacking the rearguard in the same way. Those of the Greeks in the ambush, when they were close by, rushed from the ambush and came into close combat with the enemy. The leaders and front soldiers of the pursuing Mysians suddenly came into conflict with the Greeks and were killed; and the main body, when they saw their vanguard in difficulties, fled to their villages. When Agesilaus received news of this he turned around and led his army back the same way until it met up with those in the ambush, and pitched camp where he had camped the previous day.

XXI.3 After this, the Mysians to whom the dead belonged, each sent heralds ... they took up their dead under truce. More than one hundred and thirty had been killed. Agesilaus took some guides from the

λαβὼν ἐκ τῶν] | ⁵κωμῶν τινας καθ[ηγεμόνας καὶ ἀναπαύ-
σας ....] ἡμέρας τοὺς στρ[ατιώτας ἦγεν εἰς] τὸ πρόσθεν
τ[ὸ] στράτευμα, καὶ κα[τα]βιβάσας [εἰς τὴ]ν χώραν τῶν
Φ[ρ]υγῶν, οὐκ εἰς [ἣ]ν τοῦ προτέρου [θέρ]ους ἐνέβαλεν, 690
ἀλ[λ᾿ ε]ἰς ἑ[τέ]ραν ⟨οὖσαν⟩ [ἀ]πόρ[θ]ητον, κα[κῶ]ς αὐτὴν
ἐποίει, Σπι|¹⁰[θρ]αδάτη[ν ἔχ]ων ἡγεμόνα [καὶ τ]ὸν υ⟨ἱ⟩όν.
4 ὁ δὲ Σπιθραδά[τ]ης τὸ μὲν γένος ἦν Πέρ[σης, δι]ατρί-
β..[ν] δὲ πρὸς τῷ Φαρναβάζῳ καὶ θεραπεύων [ἐκεῖ]νον,
εἶ[τα δὲ εἰς] ἔχθραν καταστὰς πρὸς αὐτόν, φοβηθεὶς μ[ὴ
κατα]ληφθῇ καὶ κακόν τι πάθῃ, παραυτίκα μὲ[ν] ἀπέ[φυ-
γεν] | ¹⁵εἰς Κύζικον, ὕστερον δ[ὲ] ὡς Ἀγη[σ]ί[λαο]ν [ἧκεν
ἄγω]ν [Με]γοβάτην υ⟨ἱ⟩ὸν νέον ὄντα καὶ καλόν. Ἀγησίλαος δὲ τούτων γενομένων ἀνέλαβεν αὐτοὺς μάλιστα μὲν
ἕνεκα τοῦ μειρακίου· λέγεται γὰρ ἐπιθυμητικῶς αὐτοῦ 700
σφόδρα ἔχειν· ἔπειτα δὲ καὶ διὰ Σπιθριδά|²⁰τ[ην,] ⟨ἡγού-
μενος⟩ ἡγεμόνα τε τῆς στρατιᾶς αὐτοῖς ἔσεσθαι καὶ
[πρὸς] ἄλλα χρήσιμον. 5 ἐκείνους μὲν οὖν τ[ο]ύτ[ων]
ἕνεκα ὑπεδέξατ[ο] προθύμως, αὐτὸς δὲ προάγων εἰς τὸ
πρόσθεν ἀεὶ τὸ στράτευμα καὶ λεηλατῶν τὴν τοῦ Φαρνα-
βάζου χώραν ἀφικνεῖται | ²⁵πρὸς χωρίον, ὃ καλεῖται Λεόν-
των Κεφαλαί. καὶ ποιησάμενος πρὸς αὐτὸ προσβολάς, ὡς
5 οὐδὲν ἐπέραινεν, ἀναστήσας τὸ στράτευμ[α] προῆγεν εἰς

---

688 τρεῖς] ἡμέρας Kalinka.
692 The papyrus reads υον.
694 προς Bartoletti; παρα Grenfell and Hunt.
[ἐκεῖ]νον, εἶ[τα Bartoletti; [αὐτὸ]ν, ἔπει[τα
Grenfell and Hunt.
698 The papyrus reads υον.
701 ⟨ἡγούμενος⟩ ἡγεμόνα Crönert;
⟨ἡγούμενος⟩ (instead of ἡγεμόνα) Grenfell
and Hunt.

villages and having rested his soldiers for ... days, he led his army forwards, and went down into the country of the Phrygians, not into the region which he had invaded the previous summer but into another area as yet unravaged, and he plundered it, having as guide Spithradates and his son.   XXI.4   Spithradates was by race a Persian, a man who lived with Pharnabazus and served him. Then having become his enemy, he feared that he would be arrested and suffer some harm, and fled at once to Cyzicus, and later came to Agesilaus, bringing with him his son Megabates, a fine young man. When this happened, Agesilaus received them, especially for the sake of the young lad, for he is said to have been extremely infatuated with him, but also on account of Spithradates to whom he thought would be a guide for his army and useful in other respects.   XXI.5 For these reasons he welcomed them enthusiastically. Leading his army forwards continually and ravaging the territory of Pharnabazus, he reached the place called Leonton Cephalae, and made attacks on it. As he was unsuccessful he moved his army and led it forward,

τὸ πρόσθε⟨ν⟩ πορθῶν καὶ λεηλατῶν τῆ[ς] χώρας τὴν ἀκέραιον. 6 ἀφικόμενος δὲ πάλιν πρὸς Γόρδιον, χω|³⁰ρίον ἐπὶ 71(
χώματος ᾠκοδομημένον καὶ κατεσκευασμένον κα⟨λ⟩ῶς,
καὶ καταζεύξας τὸ στ[ρ]άτευμα περιέμενεν ἐξ ἡμέρας,
πρ[ὸ]ς μὲν τοὺς πο[λ]εμίους προσβολὰς ποιούμενος, τοὺς
δὲ στρατιώτας ἐ[πὶ π]ολλοῖς ἀγαθοῖς συνέχων. ἐπειδὴ δὲ
βιάσασθαι τὸ χωρί|³⁵ον οὐκ ἠδύνατο διὰ τὴν Ῥαθάνου
προθυμίαν, ὃς ἐπῆρχεν αὐτοῦ Π⟨έρσ⟩ης ὢν τὸ γένος, ἀναστήσας
ἦγεν ἄνω τοὺς στρατιώτας, κελεύοντος τοῦ Σπιθριδάτου
εἰς Παφλαγονίαν πορεύεσθαι.

XXII (XVII) Μετὰ δὲ ταῦτα προάγων τοὺς Πελοποννησίους καὶ τοὺς συμμά||χους π[ρὸς τὰ ὅρια τῆς τε Φρυ-] 72
γίας καὶ τῆς Παφλαγον[ί]ας ἐκε[ῖ τὸ στράτευμα κατεσ]τρατοπέδευσε,
τὸν δὲ Σπ[ι]θριδάτη[ν πρὸς Γύην ἔπεμψε]ν·
ὁ δὲ πορευθεὶς καὶ πείσας ἐκεῖ[νον ἐπανῆκεν αὐτὸν]
ἄγων. 2 Ἀγησίλαος δὲ ποιη|¹⁵σάμεν[ο]ς [σπονδὰς ἐκ τῆς
τῶ]ν Παφλαγόνων ἀπήγα[γε] διὰ ταχ[έων τὴν στρατιὰν
ἐπὶ θ]άλατταν, φοβούμενος μ[ὴ] χειμῶν[ος τῆς τροφῆς
ἐνδέ]ωσι⟨ν⟩. ἐποιεῖτο δὲ τὴν πορε[ί]αν οὐκέτ[ι τὴν αὐτὴν
ὁδόν, ἥν]περ ἦλθε⟨ν⟩, ἀλλ' ἑτέραν, ἡγ[ού]μενος διὰ

---

711 The papyrus reads κακῶς, which does not make sense.
716 The papyrus reads πήγης (with the accent marked).
722 πρός Γύην ἔπεμψε]ν Rühl; αὐτὸν προέπεμψε]ν Grenfell and Hunt.
724—5 σπονδὰς ἐκ τῆς τῶ]ν Fuhr; σύμμαχα τὰ τῶ]ν Grenfell and Hunt.
727 The papyrus reads]ωσι.
728 The papyrus reads ἦλθε.

laying waste the unravaged part of the country. XXI.6 He arrived at Gordium, a place built on a hill and well constructed, and having encamped his army he waited six days, making attacks on the enemy and keeping his soldiers together with many comforts. When he could not take the place by force on account of the energy of Rhathanes, a Persian by race, who was in command there, he moved his forces and led them onwards, since Spithradates was urging him to march into Paphlagonia.

XXII.1 After this, he led the Peloponnesians and their allies to the borders of Phrygia and Paphlagonia and there he encamped his army, and sent Spithradates to Gyes. He went on and persuaded him and brought him back with him. XXII.2 Agesilaus made a truce with the Paphlagonians and quickly led his army towards the sea since he feared that they would be short of supplies for the winter. He did not march by the route by which he had come but another one, since he thought

[τοῦ Σαγγαρίου] διεξιρ[ῦσιν ἀκο]πῳτέρως [ἔ]|¹⁰σεσθαι
τοῖς σ[τρατιώταις. ἀπέσ]τειλε [δὲ].. ιτ[..]ρ[.]υ[...] αὐτῷ 730
Γύης το[...............]ιτ..τω.[......] ἱππέας
μ[ὲν περὶ χιλί]ους, πεζοὺς δὲ πλείου[ς δισχι]λ[ί]ων. 3 κατα-
γ[αγὼν δὲ τὸ στρ]άτευμα κατὰ Κίον τῆς Μυσίας, [πρῶ-]
τον μ[ὲν περιμείν]ας ἡμέρας αὐτοῦ δέκα κακῶς ἐ|¹⁵ποίε[ι]
τοὺς Μυσο[ὺς πάλ]ι. ἀνθ' ὧν ἐπεβούλευσαν αὐτῷ περὶ τὸν
Ὄλυμπον, [ὕσ]τερον δὲ προῆγε τοὺς Ἕλληνας διὰ τῆ[ς]
Φρυγίας τῆς παρ[αθα]λαττιδίου, καὶ προσβαλὼν πρὸς
χ[ω]ρίον τὸ καλού[μ εν]ον Μιλήτου Τεῖχος, ὡς οὐκ ἠδύνατο
λαβεῖν, ἀπῆγε [το]ὺς στρατιώτας. ποιούμενος δὲ τὴν | ²⁰πο-
ρείαν παρὰ τὸν Ῥύνδακον ποταμὸν ἀφ[ι]κνεῖται π[ρ]ὸς τὴν 740
Δασκυλῖτιν λίμνην, ὑφ' ᾗ κεῖται τ[ὸ] Δα⟨σ⟩κύλιο[ν,]
χωρίον ὀχυρὸν σφόδρα καὶ κατεσκευασμ[έ]νον ὑπὸ βασιλέως, οὗ καὶ τὸν Φαρνάβαζον ἔλεγον ἀ[ρ]γύριον ὅ[σον]
ἦν αὐτῷ καὶ χρυσίον ἀποτίθεσθαι. 4 κατεστρατοπ[ε]|²⁵δευ-
κὼς δὲ τοὺς στρατιώτας ἐκεῖθι μετεπέμπετο Πά[γ]κα-
λον, ὃς ἐπιβάτης τῷ ναυάρχῳ Χειρικράτει πεπλευκὼ[ς]
ἐπεμελεῖτο τοῦ Ἑλλησπόντου πέντε τριήρεις ἔχων. [πα-
ραγ]ενομένου δὲ τοῦ Πογκάλου διὰ ταχέων καὶ [ταῖς
τρ]ι[ή]ρεσιν εἰσπλεύσαντος εἰς τὴν λίμνην, ἐκεῖ|³⁰[νον
μὲν] ἐκέλευσεν ὁ Ἀγησίλαος ἐνθέμενον ὅσα τῶν [διηρ- 750
ποσμ]ένων ἦ⟨ν⟩ πλείονες ἄξια διαγαγεῖν εἰς τ[.]ο [.|....
περ]ὶ Κύζικον, ὅπως {αν} ἀπ' αὐτῶν μισθὸς τῷ [σ]τ[ρα-
τεύματι] γένοιτο. τοὺς δὲ στρατιώτας τοὺς ἀπὸ τῆς Μ[υ-]

---

729 τοῦ Σαγγαρίου Dugas; τῆς Βιθυνίδος
    Grenfell and Hunt.
738 The ὡς is fitted in above the line.
741 The Papyrus reads δακυλειο[.
751 εἰς τ[όπ]ον [ὀχυρὸν Crönert.
753 The τοὺς is fitted in above the line.

that the crossing of the Sangarion would be less exhausting for his soldiers. Gyes sent to him ... about one thousand cavalry and more than two thousand infantry. XXII.3 Leading his army down to Cius in Mysia, he stayed there ten days and did damage to the Mysians in retaliation for their treachery towards him near Olympus. Later he led the Greeks through coastal Phrygia and attacked the place called Miletou Teichos. He could not take it and led his soldiers away. Making his march along the Rhyndacus river he arrived at Lake Dascylitis, below which lies Dascylium, a very strong place, fortified by the King, where they said that Pharnabazus stored the silver and gold that he had.

XXII.4 He encamped his forces there and summoned Pancalus who had sailed as a marine for the admiral Cheiricrates and was guarding the Hellespont with five triremes. When the latter arrived speedily and sailed into the Lake with his triremes, Agesilaus ordered him to take on board the most valuable part of the plunder and to take ... around Cyzicus, so that from it there would be pay for the soldiers. He dismissed the soldiers

σία[ς ἀπέλυσε πρ]οστάξας αὐτοῖς ἥκειν εἰς τὸ ἔαρ, παρα-
[σκ]ευα | ³⁵[ζόμενος τ]ὸν ἐπιόντα χειμῶνα βαδίζειν εἰς
Καππα[δοκίαν, ἀκού]ων ταύτην τὴν χώραν διατείνειν
ὥσ[περ ταινία]ν στενὴν ἀρξα[μ]ένην ἀπὸ τῆς Ποντικῆς
[θαλάττης μ]έχρι Κιλικίας κ[αὶ] Φοινίκης, καὶ τ[ὸ] μῆ-
κος [αὐτῆς εἶν]αι τοσοῦτο[ν ὥσ]τε τοὺς ἐκ Σινώπ[η]ς
βαδί ‖ [ζοντας . . .   760

---

755 τὸν ἐπιόντα χειμῶνα: <τὸ ἔπιον θέρος>
Jacoby; <μετὰ> τὸν ἐπιόντα χειμῶνα?
Bartoletti; possibly παρα[σκ]ευά[ζων μετὰ] τὸν
ἐπιόντα χειμῶνα? McKechnie.

from Mysia after ordering them to come back for the spring, and prepared to go for the coming winter to Cappadocia, since he heard that this region stretched like a narrow strip, beginning at the Pontic Sea and going from there to Cilicia and Phoenicia, and that the length of it was so great that those going on foot from Sinope ...

Cairo Fragments - Commentary

In these fragments the Athenian expedition under Thrasyllus to Ephesus in 409 is being narrated. On the dating of the expedition to the summer of 409 see L. Koenen 'Papyrology in the Federal Republic of Germany and Fieldwork of the International Photographic Archive in Cairo' *Studia Papyrologica* 15 (1976), pp.39-79, at 55 and n.37. Koenen discounts Xenophon's dating of the expedition to 408/7 (*Hell.* I.2.1 and I.2.7) (under the archon Euctemon) because I.2.1 may be interpolated; he follows D.H. Hypothesis of Lysias 32 (*Diogeiton*), which puts Thrasyllus' departure in 410/9 (under the archon Glaucippus) and D.S.XIII.54.1, which puts the battle in 409/8 (under the archon Diocles). The whole papyrus consists of 82 lines. but it is in a very fragmentary condition and there are only two portions - one of about a hundred words, the other of about eighty - which can be read to make (almost) continuous sense.

Thrasyllus' activities account for all but a very small portion of Xenophon's narrative in I.2. Diodorus, by contrast, after a brief account of this expedition, gives much more detail of the Spartan recovery of Pylos in this year (XIII 64.5-7; cf. Xen. *Hell.* I.2.18), then narrates the battle in Megarian territory (D.S. XIII.65.1-2) which is the subject of the first part of the Florence fragments, and which is not mentioned by Xenophon.

The Athenians, having had two big naval victories at Cynossema and Cyzicus in 411 and 410, had voted Thrasyllus an amphibious force: 1000 hoplites, 100 cavalry and 50 triremes according to Xenophon (*Hell.* I.1.34); 30 ships, a strong force of hoplites and 100 cavalry according to Diodorus (XIII.64.1). The aim was clearly to operate against coastal areas under the control of the Spartan/Persian alliance. Thrasyllus, equipping 5000 of his sailors as peltasts, proceeded via Samos to attack Pygela (unsuccessfully), attracted Colophon's allegiance, and made a raid into Lydia (Xen. *Hell.* I.2.2-

5). These were only preliminaries. His plan was ambitious: to try to capture Ephesus. But the attack on Ephesus began seventeen days after the raid into Lydia: Tissaphernes, the Persian commander in western Asia, had had time to prepare the defence of the city.

1. attack the walls

Thrasyllus' plan was evidently complex. His forces were too small to undertake a siege, but a swift attack could often be successful against a walled city; the Thebans in 431 very nearly took Plataea (with a little inside help), failing because the Plataeans had an opportunity to organise themselves (Th. II.2.2-4): and Aeneas Tacticus offers suggestions for reducing vulnerability to attack of this sort (Aen. Tact. 2.1-8).

3. a place in Ephesian territory

Xenophon and Diodorus agree that the Athenian troops landed in two places. The passages are Xen. *Hell* I.2.7-9 and D.S. XIII.64.1.

6. Spartans

The presence of Spartans in Ephesus on this occasion is not mentioned by Xenophon or Diodorus. Koenen (p.59) suggests that the Spartan detachment was small, though he draws attention to the transfer of Spartan headquarters to Ephesus soon afterwards under Lysander's command (p.58). Notice that another token detachment of Spartans is mentioned at Florence fragments 1.1, where the author notes that twenty were killed in the engagement in Megarian territory (in this case, the account in Diodorus follows the Hell. Oxy.); the provisional inference might be drawn that the author has taken care to include details of Spartan involvement in the action of the war whenever possible.

7. with Pasion

'Pasion' is not mentioned by name either by Xenophon or by Diodorus. He should probably be identified with the Athenian general Pasiphon (Kirchner PA 11668: no known Pasion is identifiable with the officer mentioned in this passage) who is mentioned in the accounts of the treasury of Athene as one of four generals in Samos receiving state funds in 410/09 (Syll.³ 109 lines 34-36). Thrasyllus' expedition, which set out before the end of the 410/9 archon-year (see D.H. hypothesis to Lysias 32 (*Diogeiton*)), called at Samos on its way to Asia Minor (Xen. *Hell.* I.2.1). Probably Pasiphon joined the expedition as the second-in-command.

10. with Thrasyllus

Thrasyllus, a general and democratic politician, is referred to first in Thucydides' account of opposition by the forces in Samos to the oligarchy of 411 (Th.VIII.73.4): he was the hoplite general in Samos. His successful manoeuvre against a raid led by Agis up to the walls of Athens had helped persuade the Athenians to vote him the forces he had in this expedition (Xen. *Hell.* I.1.33-34). In 406 he was one of the generals executed after the infamous Arginusae trial (Xen. *Hell.* I.7.1-34: Thrasyllus (sections 29-30) was the general who planned the arrangements for picking up Athenian survivors from the sea). Diodorus (XII.64.1) mistakenly calls him Thrasybulus.

12. the harbour called Coressus

The topography of this attack on Ephesus is unclear. It had sometimes been thought before the publication of this papyrus that Coressus was a mountain rather than a harbour; though some scholars, including J. Keil whose work forms the basis of the explanation given below, had understood the name correctly before the Cairo fragment was found.

EPHESUS

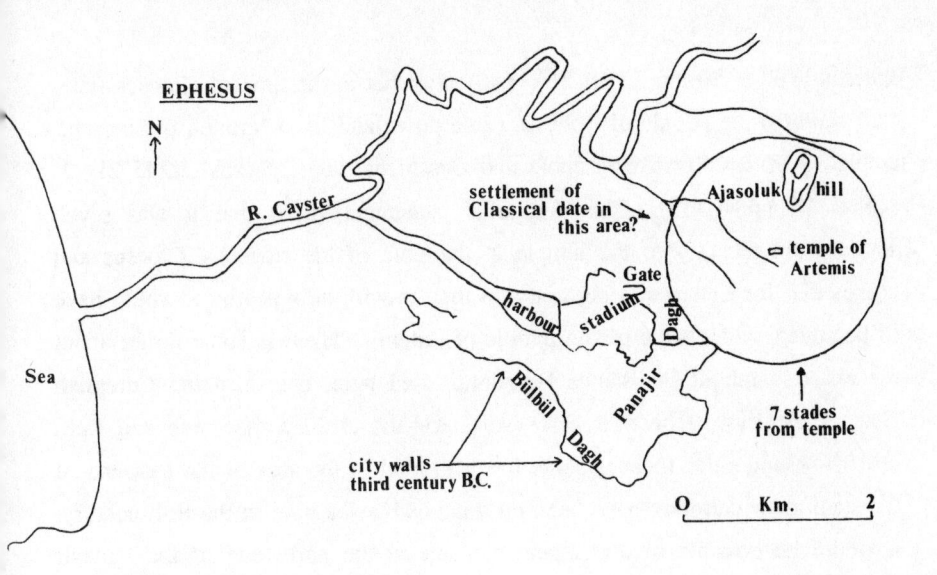

[Map showing Ephesus area with labels: R. Cayster, Sea, settlement of Classical date in this area?, harbour, stadium, Gate, Ajasoluk hill, temple of Artemis, 7 stades from temple, Bülbül Dagh, Panajir Dagh, city walls third century B.C., N arrow, scale 0-2 Km.]

16. Kil]bi[an] plain

If the letters preserved are βi and not δi, then 'Kilbian plain' is an attractive solution. The Cilbiani, who by the Augustan period were a semi-autonomous tribe whose affairs were supervised from Ephesus (Pliny *NH* V.31.120, cf. R.J.A. Talbert *Atlas of Classical History* (London and Sydney, 1985), p.158), lived well up the river Cayster but, at least at the later period for which information is available, had some connections with Ephesus including coin types showing the Ephesian Artemis (cf. P-W s.v. *Kilbianoi*). The people referred to at this point in the text may have formed the army which was gathered by Tissaphernes to defend Ephesus (Xen. *Hell.* I.2.6).

20. to the hill

The fragmentary nature of this passage is not the only hindrance to understanding where this hill was. The point is that the city at the Classical period was not where the ruins now visible stand. Lysimachus refounded

Ephesus in 286. Strabo XIV.1.21 (=640) says that at the time of Croesus (late sixth century) the people of Ephesus came down and lived 'around the present temple'. J. Keil ('Zur Topographie und Geschichte von Ephesos' *JÖAI* 21-22 (1922-24), pp.96-112) takes Herodotus' statement (I.26) that it was seven stades from the city to the temple at the time of the siege by Croesus and argues that for Ephesus to be a city on the sea with hills nearby it would have to be seven stades west of the temple of Artemis. There is some doubt about the exact length of the stades Herodotus used here; but since the Coressian Gate at the Lysimachean Ephesos was near the stadium (see map and Keil, pp.101-2), and since there is some lower ground in the area of the east end of the stadium which may have been on a navigable sea inlet in the fifth century, it would be possible to understand the area at the north end of the Panayir Dagh as being referred to.

43. were retreating

At the beginning of this second section the Ephesians are running away to somewhere, and the Athenians advance. *Koenen*, p.60 says 'in lines 40ff., soldiers flee to "strong", that is to say inaccessible, places': but there is nothing in the text to suggest that the persons reaching the inaccessible places were retreating rather than advancing. It looks as if this section may perhaps describe a stratagem whereby Timarchus and Possicrates tempt the Athenians into over-extending their attack.

46. Timarchus and Possicrates

These officers were in charge of the Ephesian forces. *Koenen* (p.60) refers to the Greek word hegemones used here as the 'official Ephesian title', but it means no more than 'officers' and cannot necessarily be taken as technical. Timarchus' name appears on Ephesian coins of the period 415-394:

B.V. Head British Museum Coin Catalogue *Ionia* (London, 1892), pp.49-50 (Ephesus nos 16 and 22).

50. trackless

The supplement *anod[euton* given in the first edition of the papyrus is rejected by H. Wankel in favour of ανοδ[ον ('Sprachliche Bemerkungen zu dem neuen Fragment der Hellenika Oxyrhynchia' *ZPE* 29 (1978), pp.54-56). His argument is that *anodeutos* is not attested before the Augustan period.

57. towards the ships in disorder

This is the final flight of the Athenians. Xenophon, in *Hell.* I.2.9 also refers to two stages in the battle, saying that the Ephesians chased some Athenians to the shore before turning their attention to others 'near the marsh'. Here it seems that some who took an upper road did worse in escaping than those who took the road to the sea; but the details are not well enough preserved for it to be clear whether this account is consistent with Xenophon's.

Florence Fragments - Commentary

I (Fragment A, Column 1)

In this column the battle fought between the Athenians and the Megarians at 'the Horns' (Nisaea) in Megarian territory in 409 is described (cf. D.S. XIII.65.1-2). The account confirms that the text of Diodorus is not defective at XIII.65.2 where twenty Spartans are stated to have been killed in the engagement. Vogel in the 1893 Teubner edition of Diodorus had emended 'Spartans' to 'Sicilians' in the account of casualties because Sicilians had been mentioned earlier and Spartans had not.

9. having ravaged the land

Diodorus makes the point that the Athenians were annoyed with the Megarians but in any case it was a normal part of ancient Greek warfare to ravage the enemy's land. See for instance W.K. Pritchett *The Greek State at War* I (Berkeley and Los Angeles, 1974), pp.53-84 (especially at pp.65-69).

13. the Athenians...were angry

The Athenians became angry with their generals more than once, and most famously after the battle of Arginusae in 406 (D.S. XIII.101.1-7; Xen. *Hell.* I.7.1-35). Arist. *Ath. Pol.* 61.1-2 describes the election of generals (most public officials in Athens were chosen by lot: Arist. *Ath. Pol.* 43.1) and the procedure for taking action against them: there is a vote in each prytany (ie. ten times a year) on the question whether the generals are doing their job well. In this case it sounds more as if there was some grumbling in Athens than as if legal action was taken against the generals because of this episode.

19. at Pylos

Sixteen years earlier (425), the Athenians had defeated the Spartans at Pylos and captured some Spartiates (Th. IV.2-41; D.S. XII.61.1-63.5). The context, given that the Athenians have just won a battle, favours the supposition that P[ylo]n should be restored here. Possibly the author makes a comment about the lack of Athenian success in the field against Spartan soldiers since the Pylos affair. If this is so, it marginally confirms the Thucydidean outlook of the author, who evidently accepts the analysis of the 431-404 war as a single war (though there is a reference to the 'Decelean War' at London Fragment 7.3) and, with Thucydides, views the Peace of Nicias as unimportant (cf. Th. VI.26.1-4).

II (Fragment A, Column 2)

Too little survives of this column for it to be possible to give any connected text. The two places where the Spartan admiral Pedaritus, who had been sent to Chios as commander by the Spartans in 412 (Th. VIII.28.5), is mentioned in this chapter, suggest that Chios is being discussed. Cratesippidas' operations there are the subject of D.S. XIII.65.3-4, the sections following those which correspond to Fragment A, Column 1 (65.1-2).

28. Pedaritus

I.A.F. Bruce 'Chios and P.S.I. 1304' *Phoenix* 18 (1964), pp.272-282, discusses this passage, which Bruce argues is a digression on Pedaritus (cf. *Bruce, ad loc.*). Digressions on particular topics are a feature of this author's style (cf. above, p.23).

Thucydides spells the Spartan admiral's name Pedaritos. Here and below the name is spelt Pedareitos. The quantity of the penultimate vowel is short in the original version (see *LSJ* s.v. eparitos), which makes it seem unlikely that the spelling change was introduced by the author - more likely a copyist introduced the intrusive epsilon. Plutarch's version of the name (Paedaretos) is a product of misunderstanding and false etymology (J. Wackernagel 'Orthographica and Verwandtes' *Philologus* 86 (1930), pp.133-144 at pp.140-141).

32. about which Thucydides also...

This is the only mention by name of Thucydides in the *Hellenica Oxyrhynchia*. It is not complete, but the restoration must be regarded as certain. The antecedent of 'which' is probably a noun qualified by a superlative adjective (of which the last three letters survive in the line above): but it is not really possible to speculate about what the noun was.

III (Fragment B, Column 1)

This poorly-preserved column probably contains some of the preliminary narrative to the battle of Notium, which forms the subject matter of Fragment B, Column 2. Many of the letters are less clear on the papyrus than are those in other columns.

40. of the King...

This is virtually certain to be a reference to the King of Persia: the use of the word *basileus* almost always has this reference in fourth century Greek: eg. at Isoc. 4(*Panegyricus*).138 and Dem. 15(*Rhodians*). 5 and 6 - indeed at section 6 of this latter speech 'when you were discussing royal affairs' (addressed to the Athenians) can perhaps be paraphrased 'you were discussing your Persian policy'.

Bruce, ad loc., suggests a reference back to Darius' decision to send Cyrus to Sardis to help the Spartans. This comes at D.S.XIII.70.3, whereas the subject matter of this column (Bruce suggests) is covered by D.S.XIII.71.1-2.

41. Clazomenae

In D.S.XIII.71.1 Alcibiades goes to Clazomenae. This, together with the presence of the definite article, makes the restoration certain.

IV (Fragment B, Column 2)

This column gives the central part of the author's narrative of the battle of Notium (407) (on which see *Bruce*, pp.35-39). This battle, a Spartan victory, was of importance as the first success of Lysander against the Athenians after his arrival in Asia (D.S.XIII.70.1-4; Xen. *Hell.* I.5.1-10 and Plut. *Lys.* 3.1-4.5), and as the battle which ended Alcibiades' second honeymoon with the people of Athens.

Athens' unexpected successes at sea after the failure of the Sicilian Expedition had been brought about, except the first of them at Cynossema in 411, at least partly by Alcibiades' efforts. But the defeat of his fleet in his own absence led to a reaction against him in Athens and to his own withdrawal from the war (D.S.XIII.74.1-3; Xen. *Hell.* I.5.16-17 and Plut. *Lys.* 5.2). The loss of a general of Alcibiades' capabilities was very serious, given Athens' already weak condition.

The accounts of the battle illustrate neatly the later use of the two contemporary traditions (Xenophon's and that of the *Hellenica Oxyrhynchia*) (see above, p. 8):

Xenophon	*Hellenica Oxyrhynchia*
	[Ephorus (not extant)]
Plutarch	Diodorus Siculus

Plutarch (*Alc.* 35.5 and *Lys.* 5.1) follows Xen. *Hell.* I.5.12 in saying that Antiochus cruised past Lysander's fleet with two ships, while the *Hell. Oxy..* and D.S.XIII.71.2 speak of a squadron of ten ships. Xenophon (*Hell.* I.5.13) and Plutarch (*Alc.* 35.6 and *Lys.* 5.1) say that Lysander at first launched a few ships, then the whole fleet when he saw Athenian reinforcements coming. The *Hell. Oxy.*, apparently, and D.S.XIII.71.3, give Lysander launching his whole fleet at once. There are other differences (the Athenians lose 15 triremes in Xen. *Hell.* I.5.14 and 22 here and at D.S.XIII.71.4) all of which are carefully explored by G. Bonamente *Studio sulle Elleniche di Ossirinco* (Perugia, 1973), at pp.35-56.

Here, for comparison, are the two accounts of Xenophon (in the *Hellenica*) and Diodorus.

1. Xen. *Hellenica* I.5.11-14

(11) But Alcibiades, hearing that Thrasybulus had come out of the Hellespont and was fortifying Phocaea, sailed over to him. He left in charge Antiochus, his own helmsman, and he told him not to sail against Lysander's fleet. (12) But Antiochus sailed from Notium with his own ship and one other to the harbour of the Ephesians; he sailed right by the prows of Lysander's ships. (13) At first Lysander launched a few of his ships and was chasing him, but when the Athenians were coming to Antiochus' help with more ships, then he drew the whole fleet up and advanced. After this the Athenians put to sea from Notium and deployed the rest of the triremes, as fast as each one could. (14) Because of this they fought the sea battle with one side in order, but the Athenians scattered - until they retreated having lost fifteen triremes. Most of the men escaped, but some were taken alive. Lysander took his ships with him, set up a trophy at Notium and sailed over to Ephesus. The Athenians went to Samos.

2. D.S. XIII.71.1-4

...he [Alcibiades] brought his ships to land at Notium and handed over his command to Antiochus, his own helmsman. He commanded him not to fight a sea battle until he returned himself; and he took his troop ships and sailed quickly to Clazomenae. This city was an ally of Athens and was suffering damage from some exiles who were ravaging the land. (2) Antiochus, though, was an impetuous character and wanted to do something outstanding by himself. He ignored Alcibiades' words and manned the ten fastest ships, telling the captains to keep the other ships ready in case a battle became necessary. He sailed over and challenged the enemy to battle.

(3) Lysander, having learnt from some deserters that Alcibiades, and with him the best of the soldiers, had gone away, thought it was his chance to do something worthy of Sparta. So he put out to sea with all his ships and sank the ship sailing at the front of the ten - Antiochus had taken this as his flagship. He turned the others to flight and pursued them, until the Athenian captains manned the other ships and came to help in no kind of order. (4) A sea battle followed, with all the ships, not far from the land; but the Athenians came off worse because of their disorganization, and they lost twenty-two ships. Some of the men in them were taken alive, but the rest swam away to the land. Alcibiades found out what had happened and turned back quickly to Notium. He manned all the triremes and sailed against the enemy's harbours. When Lysander did not dare to come out against him, he sailed to Samos.

47. to lie in wait until those of the enemy

Antiochus, the pilot of Alcibiades' flagship, who had been left in command of the fleet in Alcibiades' absence, appears to have planned to provoke Lysander to full-scale battle by enticing him out of harbour. Notium was not far from Ephesus (see map) and it might be thought extraordinary that Antiochus could manoeuvre in this way without Lysander's knowledge; but it was quite usual for armies and fleets to have very little knowledge of enemy activities, or even of the whereabouts of the enemy: cf. W.K. Pritchett *The Greek State at War* I (Berkeley and Los Angeles, 1974), pp.127-133. As far as can be judged without autopsy at Ephesus, from Admiralty Chart no. 3446, it would seem unlikely that Notium is actually visible from Ephesus or vice versa: a high cape, the Kavo Mikron Taliane (235 feet), is in the way.

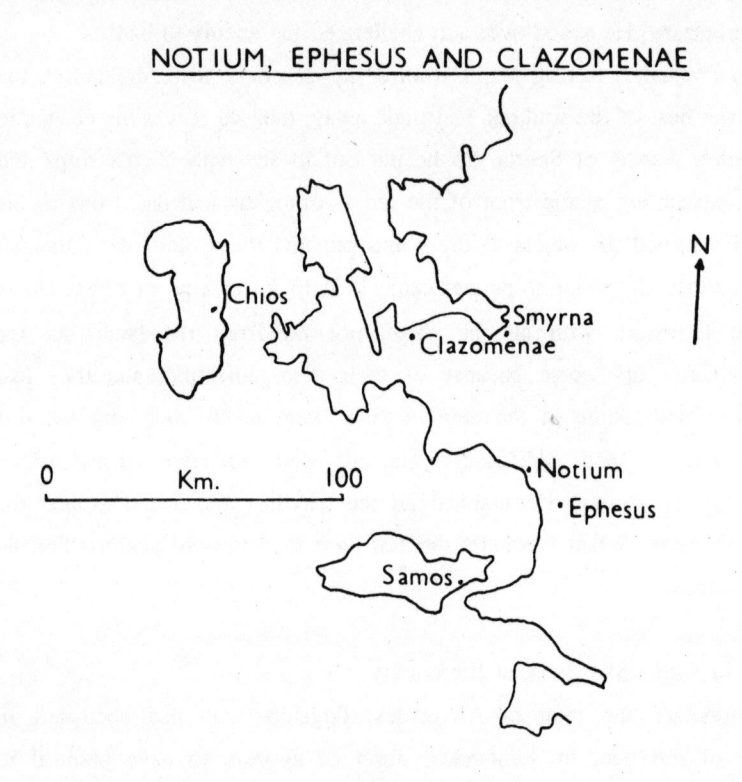

NOTIUM, EPHESUS AND CLAZOMENAE

52. they sank Antiochus

The Xenophon tradition is not specific about the stage of the engagement at which Antiochus' ship was sunk (Xen. *Hell*.I.5.13 cf. also Plut. Alc. 35.6). The account given here and at D.S.XIII.71.3 explains the Athenian defeat more adequately by noting the loss of the commander of the fleet (notwithstanding Bonamente (pp.50-52) and C. Préaux, rev. of V. Bartoletti *Nuovi frammenti delle Elleniche di Ossirinco, Chronique d'Egypte* 48 (1949), pp.348-350 at p.348).

55. Lysander

This battle, as noted above, was the beginning of Lysander's triumphant career. His honours are summed up at Plut. *Lys.* 18.1-5: he was the man who turned Sparta's potential advantage after the Sicilian Expedition into actual victory in the war.

68. twenty two ships

Préaux (*loc. cit.*) does not regard the differences in figures between the two traditions as sufficient to make it impossible to suppose that the accounts could derive from a single communiqué or journal. The wide differences of detail make this supposition implausible. The account here and in Diodorus is more convincing (*contra* Bonamente, pp.55-56).

V (Fragment C, Column 1)

In this column a guard on the wall of a besieged city lets down a rope to exchange letters with someone waiting outside the city. When and where this happened, or might have happened, is not clear from the text. The main possibilities seem to be:

(1) The siege of Thasos by Thrasybulus in 408 or 407, described very briefly at Xen. *Hell.* I.4.9 and D.S.XIII.72.1. S. Accame 'Trasibulo e i nuovi frammenti delle Elleniche di Ossirinco' *Riv.Fil.* n.s. 28 (1950), pp.30-49, argues for this.

(2) The occasion when Cratesippidas restored some exiles to Chios (409): cf. D.S.XIII.65.3-4. Bartoletti suggests this at pp.xiii-xiv of his Teubner edition. Aeneas Tacticus mentions nets, and sails with ropes, being hung over the walls of Chios on an occasion (unspecified and unknown) when Chios was betrayed (Aen. Tact. 11.3-6); but the correspondence with this account is not at all close.

(3) The siege of Byzantium by Alcibiades in 409 or 408 (*Bruce*, pp.45-46, prefers this). It is known from D.S.XIII.66.4-6, Xen. *Hell.* I.3.14-22 and Plut. *Alc.* 31 that Byzantium was betrayed to Alcibiades, and Diodorus and Xenophon in effect agree that the betrayal was arranged during the siege (sections 6 and 20, respectively), so that detail of this kind would be a credible addition; specially since Dionysius of Byzantium *De Bospori Navigatione* 13 refers to a temple of Demeter and Persephone outside Byzantium. Acceptance of this possibility involves reading Fragment C before Fragment B (there is no difficulty about this).

82. the Athenian

This is either a name (Athenaeus) or an ethnic (the Athenian). The latter seems the more likely, but there are difficulties: What was an Athenian doing as a guard on the walls of (e.g.) Byzantium? *Bruce* (p.45) suggests that if the guard was an Athenian, he was probably a deserter: but this, or any other solution, is speculative. There were mercenaries in Byzantium with Clearchus (D.S.XIII.66.5; Xen. *Hell*. I.3.15 tells a different story), so perhaps one of them happened to be (unknown to Clearchus?) an Athenian. A few years later Aeneas Tacticus was to recommend a series of elaborate measures to be taken by city governments to avoid treachery by guards on city walls (Aen. Tact. 22.1-29): incidents of this kind were a hazard.

85. the Myndian

This is probably another ethnic, though the fact that the text says 'Myndos' adds to the already severe problems. If it were not for the word 'Athenian' it would perhaps be best to treat 'Myndos' as a proper name (with De Sanctis) although there is no parallel for this: as it is, it looks as if the author is relating how an Athenian passed messages over the wall of the city to a Myndian.

86. note

If M.H. Crawford's emendation is accepted, this whole passage can be viewed as a potential or indefinite statement, referring to a plan which may never have been put into action - or not in the form indicated here. Professor Crawford has suggested to us that the author is explaining a rather complicated manoeuvre, but that the potential construction implies that this manoeuvre was not used, or proved to be unsuccessful.

London Fragments - Commentary

VI (Column 1, lines 1-27)

This chapter deals with events of 397/6. At this time, less than ten years after Athens' defeat by Sparta in the Peloponnesian War, a secret mission (recorded only here) went out from Athens with the aim of contacting Conon, the admiral of the Persian King's fleet.

1. About the same time

The extra wide margin on the left of Column 1 indicates that a new book of the author's History begins here, apparently concerned with events in 397/6. The writer adopts Thucydides' technique for synchronising events in different places: see for instance Th. II.95.1, where by means of the very expression used here Thucydides chronologically links events in Thrace and Macedonia in 429/8 with a Peloponnesian attempt on the Piraeus. We cannot tell with what events the author synchronises Demaenetus' expedition. The only clue is provided by the reference (7.1) to Pharax, the former nauarch. He commanded the Spartan forces that supported Dercyllidas' military operations in Caria, and his command seems to have ended in autumn 397, thus placing Demaenetus' activities in winter 397/6 or spring 396.

3. Demaenetus

He is mentioned by Xenophon as a general in 388/7 and 387/6 (*Hell.* V.1.26) and by Aeschines (II (*Embassy*).78). In the situation here he holds no official command but takes a state-owned trireme; and the narrative reveals that secret diplomatic dealings could take place in Athens in spite of the democratic government. This is the sort of secret action by the Council satirized at Aristophanes *Knights* 647-50. Having the support of some of the citizens, Demaenetus could apparently count (on this occasion) on the Council's backing; but the Council had to take care not to arouse the suspicions of the affluent that there was a risk of war with Sparta.

7. Conon

Conon (c.444-392) was admiral of the Athenian squadron based at Naupactus in 414, and was with the fleet operating in the Aegean and Hellespont 407-405. He escaped from the disaster at Aegospotami and found refuge with Evagoras in Cyprus. He helped to revive Persian sea power and, still in command of the Persian King's fleet, annihilated the Spartan fleet at Cnidus in 394. At the time of our narrative his headquarters was at Caunus, or possibly Rhodes.

9. Well-born and cultivated

In this passage the author refers to the upper classes in a complimentary way. The terms are loaded and indicate something of the author's political prejudice (compare the tone of 7.2).

The author has a fondness for hendiadys. In 6.2 and 6.3 parallels are drawn between 'the well-born and cultivated' and 'the moderates and men of property' on the one hand, and 'the party supporting Thrasybulus...' (not a hendiadys) and 'the majority of the populace' (literally 'the many and ordinary people') on the other (here cf. 17.1 below, with note). Distinctions are drawn between those who, being well-born and wealthy, fear the losses that would be caused by war with Sparta, and those who are associated with a more strongly democratic outlook and so are traditionally more hostile to Sparta, but who in the event refrain from risking new hostilities. Thrasybulus, son of Lycus, opposed the oligarchy of the 400 in the year 411 and was responsible for the recall of Alcibiades; banished by the Thirty, he fled to Thebes and organised the capture of Phyle (late autumn 404). Eventually he led the restoration of the democracy and later he played a prominent part in the Corinthian War. Aesimus led the return from Piraeus in 403. Anytus, general at Pylos in 410/9, was a supporter of Theramenes, was exiled by the Thirty, and returned with Thrasybulus and the democrats; an important democratic politician, he prosecuted Socrates in 399.

19. being then in a state of fear and persuaded by those who advised them...

This imputation of motive to the Athenian assembly is rather slighting, and contrasts with the approving descriptions given of the upper classes.

VII (Column 1, line 27 to Column 2 line 35)

26. The ships under Conon

Under the protection of Evagoras, King of Cyprian Salamis, Conon came to the notice of influential Persians and was appointed to command a fleet of 300 ships which was prepared in Phoenicia and Cilicia. In 397 Conon, with 40 ships, moved to Caunus in Caria and the Spartan blockade of the fleet was unsuccessful. Conon won over Rhodes, which had helped Sparta since 411, and in 394 he defeated at Cnidus a Peloponnesian fleet under the command of Pisander, the brother-in-law of Agesilaus. This Persian victory destroyed Spartan maritime power and so was much to Athens' advantage, particularly since Athens was bound by the terms of the surrender of 404 to have no more than ten (or possibly twelve) triremes.

30. who put them to death

The apparent lack of Athenian response to the execution of the envoys argues for their wish to dissociate the city from collaboration with Sparta's enemies.

32. Epicrates and Cephalus

Epicrates was one of the democrats at Piraeus in 403 and an influential politician. He was on a number of occasions accused of accepting bribes: Lysias 27 (*Epicrates*).3 mentions his acquittal on such a charge, and Plato Comicus mentions his receiving bribes from the Persian King (fr. 119). Cephalus was another democratic politician.

34. Timocrates

Timocrates the Rhodian was an agent of Tithraustes and the Persians in disseminating bribes to leaders in mainland Greek states in order to foment an anti-Spartan league (Xen. *Hell*. III.5.1). But Polyaenus says that this point of Persian policy was the idea of Conon (I.48.3). Instances and allegations of bribery were common in fourth century Greek politics, as witness Demosthenes' diatribe at 18 (*Crown*).45-49.

The point of interest here is the author's desire to show that bribes were *not* responsible for the creation of war-parties at Athens and elsewhere (contra: Xenophon (see above), whose chronology and sequence of cause and effect are rather confused). The writer is clearly intent on establishing accuracy above rumour and belief (here one might compare Thucydides' near-obsession with the mistaken Athenian tradition about the tyrannicides: I.20.2 and VI.53-59). 'some say' is unlikely to include Xenophon: our author is little, if at all, later than the Hellenica, and the reference is probably to lost works or current tradition.

42. because they treated as friends their enemies among the citizens

Since 404 (and even earlier) the Spartans had given their Boeotian allies plenty of cause for hostility; in particular, the Boeotians had wanted Athens destroyed at the end of the Peloponnesian War - Sparta's aim in not destroying Athens was to keep her as an ally, against Boeotia if necessary. Argos was traditionally an enemy of Sparta. Sparta's support for political opposition in these states is not surprising; more surprising (as *Bruce*, p.61, points out) that there was a pro-Spartan faction at all in Argos.

47. the Corinthians who wished to bring about a change of policy

Corinth was an oligarchic state. The people who wanted a democracy there achieved it eventually, about March 392 (Xen. *Hell.* IV.4.2-6), and at the same time unified Corinth, temporarily as it proved, with Argos.

50. Timolaus

The 'private grounds' are not stated. It is possible that the author did not know the details, but made an inference from Timolaus' previous friendship with the Spartans, which is strongly emphasised by the words 'outstanding pro-Spartan'. Xenophon and Pausanias claim that Timolaus (along with Polyanthes, who is not mentioned here) received Persian gold (Xen. *Hell.* III.5.1; Paus. III.9.8).

54. force of five ships

The single word translated by this expression, 'pentenaia', is paralleled by 'force of ten ships' ('dekanaia') in the Florence fragments (4.3 above).

58. Simichus

This name is an emendation. Fuhr's reason for replacing the clearly wrong name in the manuscript with 'Simichus', is the naming of one Simichus as an Athenian commander in the scholium on Aeschines II (*Embassy*).31. Unfortunately this scholium gives very little information about Simichus; but the similarity of his name to the letters in the manuscript makes the conjecture reasonable.

59. as I have said earlier

The author's statement that he has mentioned the events at Amphipolis earlier can be interpreted as indicating that he is a continuator of Thucydides, who relates the overthrow of democracy in Thasos in 411 (VIII.64.2) and the expectation of help from Sparta. Timolaus' expedition should be dated late 411. By 410 Eteonicus, a Spartan harmost, was in charge there (Xen. *Hell.* I.1.32).

61. triremes

Wilamowitz reached the figure of 11 triremes (see *apparatus criticus*) by adding up all Timolaus had obtained.

VIII (Column 2, line 35 to Column 3, line 7)

The confused condition of part of 8.2 makes an accurate interpretation of this section very difficult. Thoricus, on the east coast of Attica, is only about 40 nautical miles from Piraeus. This shows either the speed with which the Athenians responded to the emergency, or that Demaenetus was in no great haste, anticipating no hindrance from anybody except the harmosts.

IX (Column 3, line 8 to line 43)

A new year begins in this chapter. At the beginning the author uses the division of the year into summer and winter which Thucydides used (e.g. at VIII.7 and VIII.29.1) and the text goes on to discuss the state of campaigning at sea on the Asian coast.

79. at the beginning of the summer...the eighth year began

This reference to an 'eighth year' has been the cause of lengthy debate. The question is from what point the author's reckoning begins. The eighth year from the point where the author began his book is outside the range of possible dates. The passage in Diodorus dealing with Agesilaus' campaign related in the next few pages of the *Hellenica Oxyrhynchia* is placed under 396/5. This is not by itself convincing evidence that the eighth year was 396/5 and that the baseline year was 403/2 (the year of Euclides' archonship at Athens - the first year of the restored democracy after the rule of the Thirty); but it is at least a first point in favour of this date.

It was pointed out by Grenfell and Hunt (*Oxyrhynchus Papyri V* (London, 1908), pp.207-209) that since Pharax, who is referred to above (7.1) by the author as 'the former admiral', had held office in Spring-Summer 397 (Xen. *Hell*.III.2.12-14), the 'eighth year' cannot be as early as 397/6.

But the suggestion that the 'eighth year' might be 395/4 has been made and periodically restated almost since the first publication of the London Papyrus. In his chapter about Spartan admirals in *Forschungen zur Geschichte des ausgehenden fünften und des vierten Jahrhunderts* (Berlin, 1910), U. Kahrstedt makes 395/4 the 'eighth year'. More recently, G.A. Lehmann ('Spartas arche und die Vorphase des korinthischen Krieges in den *Hellenica Oxyrhynchia*' ZPE 28 (1978), pp.109-126) has argued at some length for this dating. He seeks to show that the account of the Oxyrhynchus historian must have begun before the point at which Thucydides' ends (p.110) and to suggest that the author was working within a non-Thucydidean framework (p.117) involving a classification whereby 402/1 would be the year after the end of the Peloponnesian war. He quotes D.S.XIII.8.8 (pp.119-120), where it is stated under the year 414/3 that the war begun in that year between Sparta and Athens lasted twelve years, and speculates that this piece of interpretation may come from the *Hellenica Oxyrhynchia*. But none of the specific chronological points he discusses (pp.110-117) is enough to show that 396/5 cannot have been the 'eighth year'.

RHODES AND THE CARIAN AND LYCIAN COAST

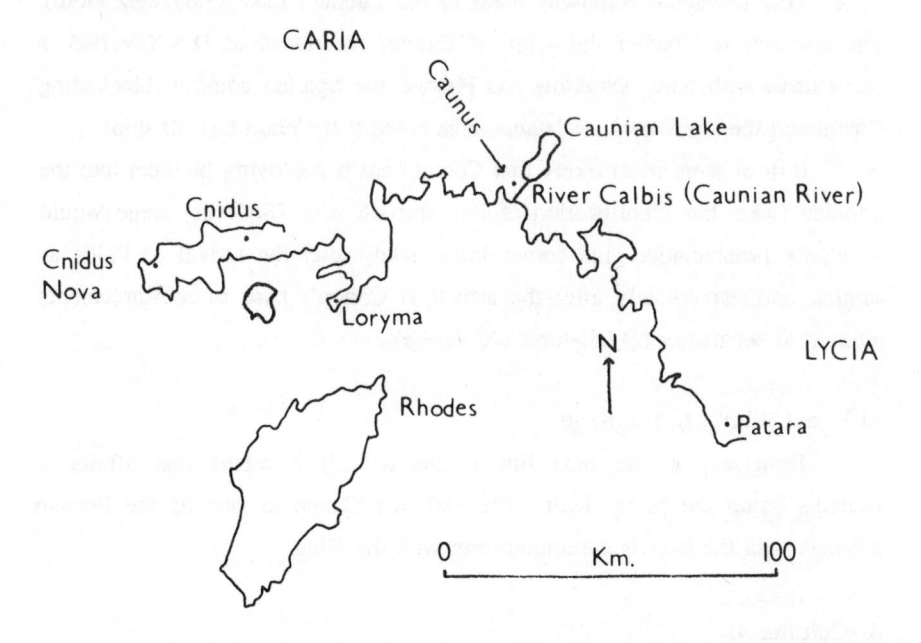

90. Pollis...as admiral

The account in D.S.XIV.79.4-8 of the naval war appears to be a compressed version of events from 398/7 to 396/5, and does not mention either Archelaidas or Pollis. For a systematic discussion of the order of events, see *Bruce*, pp.72-75.

95. the Sidonian ruler

The mention of this person, who was in command of the Phoenician ships which reached Conon, at D.S.XIV.79-8, is an indication that Diodorus' account, though it has clearly lost many other details, does ultimately derive from the *Hellenica Oxyrhynchia* at this point.

103. the river called the Caunian

This navigable waterway leads to the Caunian Lake (Köyceğiz Gölü). The question is whether the seige of Caunus mentioned at D.S.XIV.79.5 is being dealt with here. Diodorus has Pharax, the Spartan admiral, blockading Conon and the royal fleet at Caunus. It is noted that Conon had 40 ships.

It does seem most likely that Conon here is deploying his fleet into the Caunian Lake: but identification of this episode with Diodorus' siege would be highly problematic. This comes immediately after the arrival of Pollis as admiral and immediately after the arrival at Conon's base of reinforcements referred to separately by Diodorus (XIV.79.8).

110. sent [him?] to the King

Here and in the next line ('...his tent...') it seems that affairs at Conon's camp are being dealt with, and that Conon or one of the Persian officials with the fleet is communicating with the King.

X (Column 4)

Column 4 is part of the same piece of papyrus as column 3, at the bottom on the right. Higher up, column 4 is not extant at all, but it is possible to say with virtual certainty how many lines of column 4 have disappeared completely. There are no combinations of letters long enough to suggest much.

XI (Column 5, line 1 to column 6, line 27)

Fragment B, the second of the London fragments, begins at this point. There is a small but important unconnected fragment which since the first edition has been placed opposite the lower part of column 5, because of two places where letters on the fragment (fragment 3) give a plausible series of

combinations on the right-hand side of column 5: at lines 41-2...mal|lo[n...,
and at lines 47-8...A[gesi]lla[os. The particular interest of this fragment arises
from a letter delta with a line above it which is in the margin to the left of
line 45. This is probably a numeral indicating the 400th line of the papyrus
(see Introduction, p. 5). Given that a book begins at 4.1 above, and that the
columns are rightly placed (here see *Bruce*, p.67), this would indicate that 193
lines are missing after column 4 and before column 5. The subject has
changed from the struggle at sea between Sparta and Persia to Agesilaus'
campaign in Asia Minor in 395.

Chapter 11 deals with the battle in which Agesilaus' army defeated a
Persian force near Sardis. The first appearance of the *Hellenica Oxyrhynchia*
in 1908 sharpened an existing debate about the relative reliability of
Xenophon's and Diodorus' accounts of this battle and the manoeuvres leading
to it.

These, for comparison, are Xenophon's and Diodorus' accounts:

1. Xen. *Agesilaus* 1.28-33 (cf. *Hell.* III.4.20-25)

And he announced to the soldiers that he was at once going to lead
them by the quickest route to the best parts of the country, so that from there
they could prepare their bodies and minds for battle. (29) But Tissaphernes
thought he was saying this out of a wish to deceive him again, and that now
he was really going to invade Caria. So he crossed his infantry over into
Caria as before, and stationed his cavalry in the plain of the Maeander. But
Agesilaus was not lying, but he went immediately, just as he had announced,
into the area of Sardis, marched for three days through land deserted by the
enemy and provided plenty of provisions for the army. On the fourth day the
enemy cavalry came. (30) And the general told the commander of the
baggage-carriers to cross the river Pactolus and encamp. But they, seeing the

THE SARDIS CAMPAIGN 395 B.C.

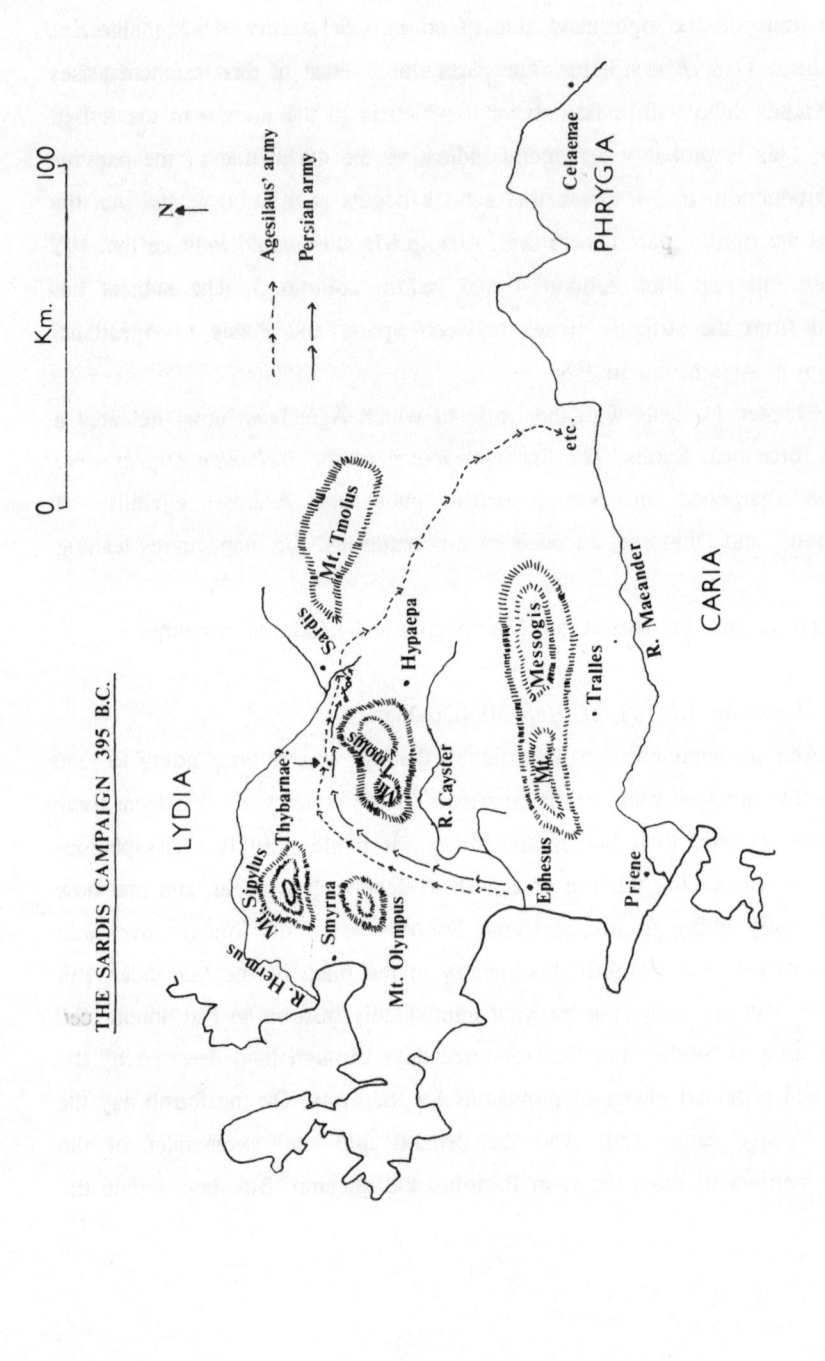

- - -> Agesilaus' army
⟶ Persian army

Greeks' camp-followers spread out for plunder, killed many of them. Noticing this, Agesilaus ordered the cavalry to give help. But the Persians when they saw the assistance, gathered together and drew up the full ranks of their cavalry. (31) Then Agesilaus, realising that the enemy's infantry was not yet there, but none of his forces was absent, thought it was the right time to join battle if he could. So he sacrificed and led his column against the cavalry drawn up against them, and he ordered the ten youngest age classes of hoplites to run forward to close quarters, and he told the peltasts to follow on at a run. And he ordered the cavalry to attack, with him and the whole army following. (32) The best of the Persians met the cavalry attack: but when the full pressure was on them they broke, and some fell right away in the river [Pactolus], and the others ran away. But the Greeks followed and captured their camp too. And the peltasts turned to plunder, of course: but Agesilaus encamped in a circle having everything, friend and enemy, inside the perimeter.

2. D.S.XIV.80.1-4

After this Agesilaus led out his army into the plain of the Cayster and the land around Sipylus and plundered the property of the inhabitants. But Tissaphernes collected up 10,000 cavalry and 50,000 infantry, followed the Spartans and killed those who straggled from the column on foraging expeditions. Agesilaus, drawing up the soldiers into a hollow-square formation, kept to the foothills of Sipylus, waiting for a suitable time to attack the enemy. (2) And reaching the land near Sardis he ravaged the gardens and the estate of Tissaphernes, which was extravagantly laid out, with plants and other things, for luxury and the enjoyment of good things in peace. Turning back afterwards, when he got half way between Sardis and Thybarnae, he sent Xenocles the Spartiate with 1400 soldiers by night into a certain shady place, so that he might ambush the barbarians. (3) He himself set out at daybreak with the army, and when he passed the ambush and the barbarians were attacking in a disorderly way and harrassing those in the rear, he suddenly and unexpectedly turned round against the Persians. When the fight became fierce and the signal to those who were in ambush had been raised, they sang the paean and charged the enemy, and the Persians, seeing that they were caught in the middle, were struck with panic and immediately ran away. (4) But Agesilaus' men followed them for some distance, killed more than 6,000, collected a large number of prisoners, and plundered the camp, which was full of many good things.

There are large differences between these two accounts, so that it has even been doubted whether they describe the same battle (see for example, G.L. Cawkwell rev. of *Bruce* C.R. n.s.18 (1968), pp.288-290). The *Hellenica Oxyrhynchia* account, though very fragmentary in the part dealing with the march, has the same main features as Diodorus' account - in particular the ambush set by Agesilaus and commanded by Xenocles. There are, though, differences between the *Hellenica Oxyrhynchia* and Diodorus: the numbers killed by the Greeks vary by a factor of ten, and the episode of raiding Tissaphernes' estate cannot be identified as being present in the *Hellenica Oxyrhynchia*.

The differences between the *Hellenica Oxyrhynchia*/Diodorus accounts and the account given by Xenophon are much more fundamental. It is now generally, though not perhaps universally, agreed that Xenophon's 'shortest route to the best parts of the country' probably denotes the route towards Sardis via the Karabel pass, rather than the route up the Cayster valley, then north from Hypaepa. On this see J.K. Anderson 'The Battle of Sardis in 395 B.C.' *CSCA* 7 (1974), pp.27-53, at pp.33-41.

The question of what sort of battle was fought and where is less tractable. In Xenophon Agesilaus marches three days without enemy interference; in the other accounts the Persians track the Spartan army. In Diodorus, and presumably in the *Hellenica Oxyrhynchia*, Agesilaus' army turns back west before fighting between Sardis and Thybarnae (on Thybarnae see L.A. Botha *The Hellenica Oxyrhynchia and the Asiatic Campaign of Agesilaus* (M.A. thesis, Univ. of S. Africa, 1980), p.68, where it is argued that Thybarnae is the same place as the Thymbrara referred to by Xeonophon at *Cyropaedeia* VII 1.45 and 2.11, and suggested that it may have been at the site of the modern Turğutlu, 35km or so west of Sardis), but in Xenophon Agesilaus' army seems to be facing towards Sardis. This difference is hard to explain. As G. Busolt noted as early as 1908, a composite account is not possible here: the decision which must be made is which of Xenophon and the writer of the *Hellenica Oxyrhynchia* is more likely to be right (G. Busolt 'Der neue Historiker und Xenophon' *Hermes* 43 (1908), pp.255-285, esp. at pp.255-260).

Recent work has tended to favour the view that Xenophon is right. J.K. Anderson provides arguments to support the view that Xenophon was present on Agesilaus' expedition in 395 (J.K. Anderson 'The Battle of Sardis in 395 B.C.' *CSCA* 7 (1974), pp.27-53, at pp.30-32). V.J. Gray argues for a view of the Oxyrhynchus historian as a writer who believed detail important for its own sake and who may have fabricated details in this account. She draws attention to his liking for stratagems, and gives a list (V.J. Gray 'Two different approaches to the battle of Sardis in 395 B.C.' *CSCA* 12 (1979), pp.183-200): see Introduction above, p.16, n.1.

But the point is not definitively settled. C. Dugas argued in favour of the *Hellenica Oxyrhynchia* in 1910 (C. Dugas 'La Campagne d'Agésilas en Asie Mineure' *BCH* 34 (1910), pp.58-95) and asked the pertinent question what the purposes of Agesilaus' campaign were (p.73): this is rather easier to answer from the *Hellenica Oxyrhynchia* account, where it appears as a speculative plundering operation, than from Xenophon, who gives an elaborate account of the preparations, for what seems to be intended as a decisive push (Xen. *Ages.* 1.25-28; *Hell.*III.4.16-19) but ends rather ineffectively.

125. the plain] of the Ca[ys]ter...

This seems to be the moment when Agesilaus and his army set out. The word for 'plain' is restored following Diodorus.

130. Tissaphernes...followed the Greeks...

Comparison between Xenophon and Diodorus reveals contradiction about where Tissaphernes was in the early part of the Sardis campaign. Xenophon does not specify where Tissaphernes was when he directed his forces to Caria (Xen. *Hell.*III.4.21; *Ages.*1.29), but says after giving his version of the battle that Tissaphernes was in Sardis at the time of the battle (Xen. *Hell.*III.4.25). Diodorus has Tissaphernes withdrawing from the battle into the city of Sardis (D.S.XIV.80.5). He is evidently following the account given here whereby Tissaphernes took personal charge of his army in this operation.

161. Delta (in margin)

The letter delta in the left-hand margin at column 5, line 45 may indicate the 400th line copied by the scribe. See Introduction above, p 5.

195. the majority were cavalry and troops without armour

Xenophon says quite unambiguously that the Persian force had no infantry with it (Xen. *Ages.*1.31; *Hell.*.III.4.23). Diodorus, on the other hand, has Tissaphernes leading 10,000 cavalry and 50,000 infantry (D.S.XIV.80.1): this reference corresponds to the fragmentary numerals given in 11.3 above, though Diodorus' numbers are not the same as the ones given by the *Hellenica Oxyrhynchia*. There are no strong *a priori* grounds for preferring one version over the other. Perhaps Xenophon was there, and would know; perhaps, on the other hand, it seems odd that a Persian force of cavalry, with no infantry, should engage Agesilaus' army rather than withdraw into Sardis.

XII (Column 6, line 27 to column 7, line 4)

In this chapter, the author describes Agesilaus' follow-up to his victory outside Sardis. Neither Diodorus nor Xenophon describes this continuation of the expedition. Agesilaus does not attempt an attack on Sardis itself, but goes on a pillaging march as far as the river Maeander, followed at a distance by Tissaphernes' army. His likely route is marked on the map above.

221. from Celaenae, which is the greatest city in Phrygia, and it flows out to the sea near Priene...

The author gives an idea of the course of the river Maeander, and goes on to mention the possibility of an attack on Celaenae, at the river's source. But an attack on a city would have been a difficult undertaking for Agesilaus' army: they had already avoided attempting to capture Sardis.

225. Made a sacrifice to find out whether he should cross the river or not...

The Spartans are often recorded as having sacrificed to discover whether to proceed on campaign or not (see *Pritchett III* pp.67-71). These sacrifices were a routine part of Spartan procedure, and in fact in Thucydides are only mentioned in cases where they proved unfavourable (*Pritchett* III, p.69). Pritchett warns against interpretations which assume that the purpose of the divination was to give sanction to decisions reached beforehand and on rational grounds. In contrast *Bruce*, pp.87-8, mentions some possible arguments for not proceeding across the Maeander in this case: chiefly that going towards Celaenae would involve more risk and less plunder than going down towards the coast on the north side of the river.

XIII (Column 7, line 4 to end of column 8)

Some of the few words which can be read in this chapter (the King, Tissaphernes, the Greeks, Tithraustes, Ariaeus) give the clue to its content: it deals with how Artaxerxes, hearing of Tissaphernes' failures, appointed Tithraustes commander of the army in western Asia Minor, and how Tithraustes had Tissaphernes' head cut off. This story is told by Diodorus at XIV.80.6-8 and more briefly by Xenophon at Hellenica III.4.25. The length of the account in this chapter suggests considerable detail: evidently the political manoeuvres involved were complex. Polyaenus (VII.16.1) tells a story in which Ariaeus on instructions received by letter summons Tissaphernes to Colossae and, with bath attendants' help, arrests him while he is in the bath. He then hands him over to Tithraustes who takes him in a closed wagon to Celaenae before beheading him and sending the head to the King. It is possible that the *Hellenica Oxyrhynchia* may be the source of this account.

Ka]teren eis 'swooped down on' is a phrase which occurs again in 21.1.

XIV (Columns 9 and 10)

At this point we enter Fragment C, which is not necessarily particularly close in the author's work to the end of Fragment B (but see below on Chapter 16, p.153). This chapter is particularly broken, but seems to involve a character sketch of some person, who is described (col.10 line 21) as 'very democratic' and is said a little earlier to have 'handled [affairs] very well'.

The most likely candidates as the subject of this analysis seem to be Agesilaus and Cyrus, though other names have been mentioned (see *Bruce*, p.93). Sparta (or Spartans) seems to be mentioned in fragment no.10, which apparently goes with column 10, but this need be no hindrance to Cyrus' being the person discussed. 'of the dynasts' (unless introduced for contrast, rather than, as the restored text suggests, for comparison of like with like) might seem to be a class into which Cyrus would fit better than Agesilaus.

In favour of Agesilaus there is the position of the chapter in the book (though the break before column 9 dilutes the force of this point) and the sequence of events in Diodorus, where Tithraustes makes a truce with Agesilaus after the death of Tissaphernes. It would seem a little soon after his arrival on the scene for the author to be giving a verdict on Tithraustes.

XV (Column 11, lines 1-34)

Here a democratic *coup d'état* in Rhodes in 395 is described. This *coup* was unknown before the discovery of the *Hellenica Oxyrhynchia*, as it is not mentioned in the accounts of Xenophon or Diodorus.

Rhodes, a Doric-speaking island which had been in the Delian league, had a number of revolutions, successful and unsuccessful, in the late fifth and early fourth centuries. There was an attempt at revolution in 411, when Rhodes (having revolted from Athens in 413) was on Sparta's side and not yet united as a single *polis* (D.S. XIII.38.5): the synoecism took place in or about 408 (D.S. XIII.75.1), presumably under an oligarchic constitution. In 396 the Rhodians expelled the Spartan fleet to admit Conon (D.S. XIV.79.6).

A few years after the events dealt with here, in 391, the oligarchs brought about a counter-revolution (Xen. *Hell.* IV.8.20-25; D.S. XIV.97.1-4 and 99.4-5; see H.D. Westlake 'Rival Traditions on a Rhodian Stasis' *MH* 40(1983), pp.239-250), and there was still further unrest in 357.

The account in this chapter is dated to 395 because it is in the same summer as the events described in chapter 16.

348. he reviewed the soldiers

As becomes clear further on (15.3), this is said about Conon. At this stage of the campaign he is keeping the Persian fleet in training in its new base of Rhodes.

349. the pretext being...but in fact wanting...

A change of government in Rhodes was the goal of Conon's policy, according to the author. The narrative is too fragmentary to make it clear why the present régime, which had admitted his ships after expelling the Spartans', should be considered unsatisfactory. If the reason is taken to be the general Athenian preference for democracy (cf. [Xen.] *Ath.Pol.* 3.10-11), then the incident would show Conon as furthering Athenian interests in a quite direct way before the battle of Cnidus. It is worth noting that this motive is ascribed to Conon at D.S. XIV.39.3, in the passage where he accepts the naval command from the King of Persia.

355. not wanting to be there at the overthrow of the government

It has been suggested that Conon's regard for some of the Rhodian oligarchy may have been a factor in prompting him to leave Rhodes at the moment of the *coup* (*Bruce*, pp.98-99); but Bruce's other comment (p.99), that Conon may have wished to avoid seeming to be connected with a failed attempt against the government, is more perceptive. His policy goal is secured at someone else's risk.

356. Hieronymus and Nicophemus

These men were both Athenian citizens (Kirchner *PA* 7552 and 11066), whom Conon again put in charge of the fleet in his absence in the next year when he went to see the King of Persia (D.S. XIV.81.4). Harpocration records that Hieronymus became an Athenian general (it is not known when) and that he was referred to by Ephorus in his eighteenth and nineteenth books (=*FGrHist* 70 (Ephorus) F73).

363. time to undertake the deed, they gathered with daggers

The word play *encheirein* (to undertake)/*encheiridiois* (with daggers) seems hardly likely to be accidental, and is matched a little further on by *boesantos* (shouting)/*boetheian* (help), another pair of similar-sounding words with different meanings. The historic present *apokteinousi* (they kill[ed]), is another feature showing that this is intended to be a vivid narrative passage.

367. Dorimachus...said 'Citizens! Let's go for the tyrants as quick as we can!'

This piece of direct speech (the only one in the extant part of the work) is a further vivid feature for this passage telling the story of the overthrow of the Rhodian oligarchy. Nothing is known of Dorimachus apart from this reference.

370. Diagorean family

The family of Diagoras, whose success at boxing in the Olympic Games of 464 B.C. was celebrated by Pindar in *Olympian* 7, had been, it seems, the leading family of Rhodes up to the time of this democratic *coup d'état*.

373. as soon as they were assembled

In these last two sentences of the chapter the author is continuing to use language carefully to produce a dramatic effect. He has Conon arrive back just as the meeting gets under way, and uses *heke* (came), a simple word with some poetic overtones, to describe this arrival. This is clearly deliberately colourful writing, and the word *sphage* (slaughter) adds to the effect. The final sentence rounds off the chapter with a convincing clarity, using the technical-sounding word *epanastasis* (internal revolution: cf. *Bruce* p.102).

XVI (Column 11, line 34 to column 12, line 31)

Chapters 16 to 18 focus on Boeotia and provide much the most detailed source available on the constitution and politics of Boeotia in the late fifth and early fourth centuries. This is particularly valuable since Thebes and Boeotia were under an oligarchic government. Knowing something about it allows some contrasts and interesting parallels with Athens, about which more information is available. Sparta might also be classified as an oligarchy (if the Spartan constitution is classifiable) but was clearly much less like an ordinary oligarchy than Boeotia.

J.A.O. Larsen argues that, for understanding Greek thought and institutions of the fifth century B.C., the oligarchy of Boeotia is nearly as important as the democracy of Athens ('The Boeotian Confederacy and Fifth-Century Oligarchic Theory' *TAPA* 86 (1955), pp.40-50 at p.40). Oligarchy was certainly as typical a form of government in Greece at this period as democracy.

The constitution described is the one which was established after the ending in 447 of Athenian control of Boeotia (which had lasted since 457) and which was followed until the Peace of Antalcidas (King's Peace) of 387. In the debate between the Plataeans and Boeotians, after the siege of Plataea near the beginning of the Peloponnesian War, in front of the Spartans, the Boeotian speaker implicitly contrasts this constitution with the 'ruling group of a few men' who were in charge of Boeotia at the time of the Persian invasion (Th. III. 62.3).

There is no trace in the description of this constitution of a Boeotian assembly (see R.J. Bonner 'The Boeotian Federal Constitution' *C.Phil*.5 (1910), pp.405-417, at p.411, and H. Swoboda 'Studien zur Verfassung Boeotiens' *Klio* 10 (1910), pp.315-334 at p.318). Such a thing was not inconceivable: the Arcadian League set up in 370 had an assembly of 10,000 (D.S. XV.59.1). Its absence, and the fact that all the power was held by relatively small councils, forms the most distinctively oligarchic feature of the Boeotian constitution. Election of magistrates by vote was regarded, by Aristotle at least, as an aristocratic (*Politics* 1273 b40) or oligarchic (1294 b9) procedure, because the rich were better placed to attract votes.

379. This summer

As the papyrus fragment is continuous at this point, this synchronizes the events of this chapter with those of chapter 15. In Diodorus the account of the Boeotian-Phocian war (XIV.81.1-3) follows immediately after the appointment of Tithraustes as satrap and the execution of Tissaphernes (the material of chapter 13 above). The year of these events, as of the Sardis Campaign and the Rhodian *coup*, is 395.

380. Those chiefly responsible for the bad relations...

The author brings in his introductory material on the constitution and politics of Boeotia cleverly. After just a sentence mentioning the war with the Phocians, enough to make clear the relation of what follows to the line of narrative of the historical work, he focuses on the position in Boeotia. This smooth transition, well signalled to the reader, is a good illustration of the author's technique in the use of digression (on which see *Bruce*, pp.11-15).

381. Not many years previously

This seems to refer to the same events which are mentioned below in 17.2 as happening 'a little while before'. There it is made clear that the 'political reversal' (*stasiasmon*) referred to here was a change in the faction controlling the government, rather than any change in the constitutional system. See the note below on 17.2, p.34.

383. At that time the situation in Boeotia...

Xenophon says that in 387 the Thebans were forced to accept the terms of the King's Peace and let the Boeotian cities become autonomous (*Hell.* V.1.33); 'at that time' implies that this account was written after this change had taken place, and so gives a date before which this history cannot have been written. See Introduction, above, p. 10.

The constitution described here appears to be the one set up in 447 after the battle of Coronea and the defeat of Athens. Thucydides appears to be definite in saying that the Athenians were actually in control in Boeotia after the victory of Oenophyta in 457 (Th.I.108.3) but it is much less clear what system or systems of government they sponsored: the point is discussed by N.H. Demand (*Thebes in the Fifth Century, B.C.* (London, 1982), pp.32-36).

384. There were four councils established at that time in each of the cities...

The four-council system was an oligarchic system and a system for making decisions by initial consideration followed by ratification. The explicitly oligarchic nature of the arrangement is made clear by the provision that not all citizens could serve on the councils, but only those who met what the author describes vaguely as 'a certain property qualification'. The suggestion that this may have amounted to a hoplite census (cf. *Bruce*, p.104) is obviously plausible.

Aristotle's *Constitution of the Athenians* refers to a proposal at Athens in the confused days of the 411 oligarchic *coup d'état* which would have set up in due course a system of four councils, which would apparently have sat in turn (Arist. *Ath.Pol.* 30.3). Though this plan does not seem to correspond exactly to the Boeotian system of decision making by stages, it is very interesting that sponsors of antidemocratic change in Athens should choose an arrangement so reminiscent of the Boeotian structure. J.A.O. Larsen points to the Boeotian and Athenian four-council plans as 'part of a more extensive oligarchic movement' ('The Boeotian confederacy and Fifth Century Oligarchic Theory' *TAPA* 86 (1955), pp.40-50, at p.47).

Two points should be noted in this connection. First that the series of arrangements including the four-council system was not implemented in the short months of the 411 *coup*: it was explicitly intended for the future (*Ath.Pol.* 31.1) - and perhaps, by some more cynical plotters, merely as window-dressing to appeal to the broad range of comparatively well-off citizens who could be expected to respond with enthusiasm to the idea of 'turning over the...government to those best able to serve with bodies or property...' (*Ath.Pol.* 29.5); this strengthens the suggestion that it was a feature of a theory-based system. Second that the oligarchy behind the *coup d'état*, wanting to keep power in their own hands, avoided setting up the assembly of 5,000 which was supposed to be the new sovereign body (Th.VIII.92.11, *Ath.Pol.* 33.2 and cf. Lysias 20 (*Polystratus*).13): though promises had been necessary to attract support, the ideas of the oligarchy, here as in Boeotia, ran on the lines of governing without a large deliberative assembly.

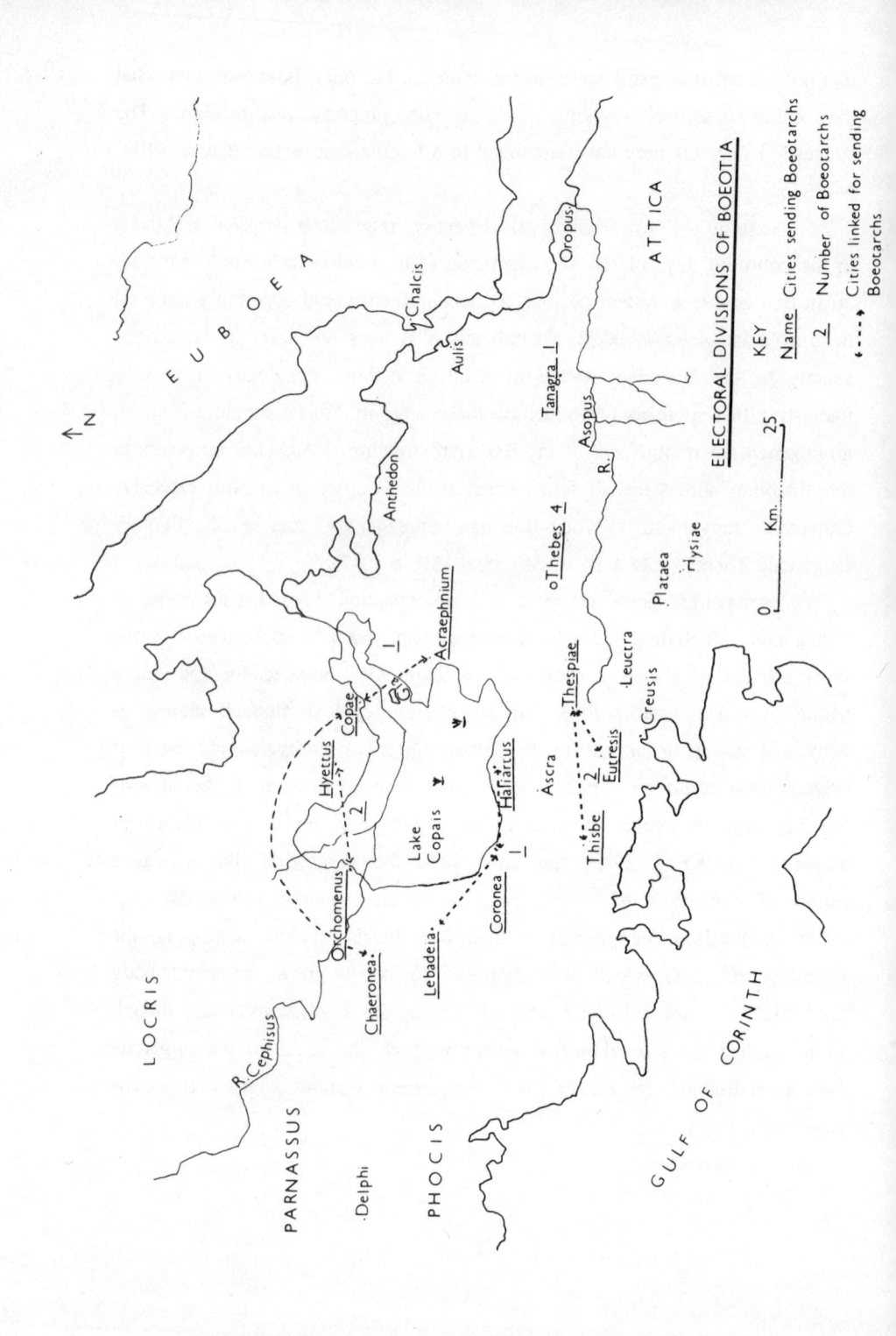

390. their internal affairs...

It is usually thought that the Boeotian federal council was of the same four-part type as the local councils. The Oxyrhynchus author is perhaps a little bit ambiguous here as to whether the local councils' arrangements applied at the federal level, but the reference to 'the four councils of the Boeotians, which have all the power' at Th.V.38.2, makes the picture clearer. Arguing against Grenfell and Hunt's view that the federal council was not in four parts, R.J. Bonner notes that the choice is between a statement of Thucydides and a silence of the Oxyrhynchus historian ('The Four Senates of the Boeotians' (*C.Phil.* 10(1915), pp.381-385, at p.384). The fact that the whole system has the appearance of a structure deliberately worked out and implemented at a particular time to supersede previous arrangements, tends to support the presumption that the pattern of organization of city councils could be the same as the pattern of the federal council.

392. All who lived in that area were arranged in eleven divisions...

The map links up the places attested by the author as being connected for the election òf Boeotarchs. Wilamowitz was the first to note that 'Hysiaeans' must be the inhabitants of Hyettus, to the north of Lake Copais, and not the inhabitants of Hysiae, near Plataea (*Oxyrhynchus Papyri* V (London, 1908), p.227). Hyettus was probably under the control of Orchomenus at this period (cf. *Bruce*, pp.106-7): this grouping supplied two Boeotarchs.

There were two groupings, of three cities each, each providing one Boeotarch - one of these groupings to the south and west of Lake Copais, the other stretching round the north side of the lake, to both sides of Orchomenian territory. Down towards the south coast of Boeotia was the grouping dominated by Thespiae ("The Thespians with Eutresis and Thisbe'), and to the east of Thebes, Tanagra provided one Boeotarch.

With Plataea under Theban control and its right to return Boeotarchs being exercised by Thebes, the weight of influence in the administration of Boeotia must have been with Thebes (here cf. N.H. Demand *Thebes in the Fifth Century B.C.* (London, 1982), pp.37-38, arguing that from the outset and before the war between Thebes and Plataea the whole point of the federal political structure was to give Thebes effective control). There is some evidence that in earlier periods Orchomenus and Tanagra had been able to follow a political path distinct from Thebes' (cf. *Bruce*, pp.106-7), and Thespiae was from time to time a centre of opposition to Thebes (cf. Th.IV.133.1 and VI.95.2); but at this date it is clear that Boeotian policy is in effect the policy of the ruling party in Thebes.

404. They provided sixty councillors per Boeotarch...

G. Glotz explains the arithmetical calculation which brought the size of the council to 660: the total had to be divisible (he argues) in the first place by 11 (the same number of councillors per Boeotarch), in the second place by 4 (because of the four-council system), in the third place by 3 (to allow equal representation in the groupings of three states linked for returning Boeotarchs), in the fourth place by 5 (this to account for the grouping '...Scolus, Erythrae, Scaphae and the other places...' which seems to account for the fourth Theban Boeotarch: Glotz supposes that there were two 'other places'). The need for the total to be divisible by 2 (to accommodate the Orchomenus-Hyettus grouping) is of course dealt with by the fact of 4 being in the calculation anyway, so that the rigmarole runs:

$$3 \times 4 \times 5 \times 11 = 660$$

(cf. G. Glotz 'Le conseil fédérale des Béotiens' *BCH* 32 (1908), pp.271-278, at pp.277-8).

As far as can be judged from the comparatively little that is known about the population of the cities of Boeotia, the divisions of the country seem probably to have been of sizes at least roughly proportional to the numbers of Boeotarchs and councillors they returned. Thebes was clearly much the largest city. There is a scatter of pieces of evidence about the size or military strengths of Boeotian cities, relating to dates from the early fifth to the early second centuries B.C., collected by K.J. Beloch in *Die Bevölkerung der griechisch-römischen Welt* (Leipzig, 1886) at pp.161-172, which cannot really be summarized in the space available here, but with some caution, one comparison may be useful: from late third century ephebic inscriptions, recording the names of twenty-year old men completing their military training, which exist for eight Boeotian towns (Chaeronea, Lebadeia, Orchomenus, Hyettus, Copae, Chorsiae, Acraephia and Thespiae), Beloch calculates the combined army strengths of these places at that date at 6,160 (p.171); and Diodorus (XVII.14.1) records that in 336 when Alexander captured Thebes over 6,000 Thebans were killed, with 30,000 taken prisoner (cf. *Beloch* p.166) - those killed being presumably the soldiers. If the periods are taken as comparable and an allowance made for the four cities mentioned by the Oxyrhynchus author and not represented by ephebic lists (Coronea, Thisbe, Eutresis, Tanagra), then, assuming no significant shift in population structure, the electoral position of Thebes might seem to match its size reasonably well.

405. and they paid their daily expenses

Modern scholars have failed to agree on whether this means that the government or the councillors themselves paid the expenses. The question is quite important. R.J. Bonner ('The Boeotian Federal Constitution' *C.Phil.* 5 (1910), pp.405-417 at p.407) assumes that the government paid and uses this assumption to argue that the oligarchic system of Boeotia was based on a hoplite franchise such that adult men who could afford to arm themselves as heavy infantrymen could vote, and be candidates for seats on the council. J.A.O. Larsen agrees about the government paying (*Representative Government in Greek and Roman History* (Berkeley and Los Angeles, 1955), p.205, n.33) but G. Glotz (art.cit. p.272) and P. Cloché (*Thèbes de Béotie* (Namur, 1952), p.73) both argue that the councillors must have paid. If this were so, it would restrict membership of the council far more tightly, even if (as *Bruce*, p.108, suggests) the council members had to spend only a quarter of the year living on unearned income.

autoi ('they') is masculine and there is a certain awkwardness about taking its antecedent to be *ta mere* ('the electoral divisions'). But a literal translation of the clause in question is 'and for-these-men they used to pay out the-things for the day': taking *toutois* ('for-these-men') as referring to the same people as *autoi* ('they') really presents more difficulty than the alternative.

Not knowing how often one was permitted to serve on the council, it is not really possible (even assuming that the state paid expenses) to work out what proportion of the enfranchised citizens might at some time serve. H. Swoboda attempts some calculations, which if correct would suggest that over a period of years perhaps 3,000 or so Thebans, 1,500 or so Orchomenians or Thespians, might take part ('Studien zur Verfassung Boeotiens' *Klio* 10 (1910), pp.315-344, at pp.320-321).

406. For the organization of the army

Here the author mentions a number of areas (including military service, taxation, jury service) administered via the electoral divisions. This points up how the artificial and carefully thought out constitution acted as an instrument of social control, rather as Cleisthenes' reforms to the Athenian tribal system, and introduction of demes, advanced democracy by creating new loyalties and weakening the divisive force of the older arrangements.

413. the Cadmea

Named after Cadmus, the city's legendary founder, the Cadmea was the citadel at the heart of Thebes.

XVII (Column 12 line 31 to column 14 line 6)

414. the best and most notable of the citizens...

Again a hendiadys (cf. 6.2-3 above) and again a phrase complimentary to the upper classes. The author is careful to define the Boeotian political struggles as taking place within the oligarchic class (and indicates impartiality on the points at issue, as the next note but one shows). This contrasts with the position he takes in 6.2-3, where he more or less openly endorses upper class attitudes in Athens at the time of Demaenetus' voyage and speaks with implicit scorn about the motivations of the majority.

419. Leontiades' party supported the Spartans

This well-constructed sentence follows the chiastic 'a, b:b, a' pattern. After naming the leading figures (he chooses to give three on each side) he picks up first the second group named and gives detail.

Twelve years later in 383 Ismenias and Leontiades (the two first named) were still at the head of their respective parties. Leontiades arranged Phoebidas' capture of the Cadmea in that year: he had Ismenias arrested (Xen. *Hell.* V.2.28-31). The others mentioned by the author appear to be less important figures, except perhaps Androcleidas, whom the Spartans later charged with being jointly responsible, with Ismenias, for 'all the trouble and disorder in Greece' (i.e. the Corinthian War; Xen. *Hell.* V.2.35). Details of possible identifications of Antitheus with a figure called Amphitheus or Amphithemis, and of Asias with one Archias, are given at *Bruce*, pp.110-111: so are arguments for emending 'Corrantadas' to 'Coeratadas'. But three names out of six seems a high proportion to have to change. Much more likely the author for literary reasons wanted three leaders for each side. Putting the names down conveys an impression of substance - the detail helps the reader feel he has engaged with the material. Notice that for variation the author uses two leaders from each side at the end of 17.2. But it is quite likely that some of the names given belong to people not important enough to appear elsewhere in extant texts.

420. Ismenias' party was accused of supporting the Athenians

The author stresses that despite their kindness towards the pro-democratic exiles from Athens in 404, Ismenias and his followers were not pro-Athenian. But they clearly took an anti-Spartan line over a number of years (see previous note, and also 18.1 below). By making, and implicitly endorsing, the distinction between this and being pro-Athenian, the author invites the reader to regard him as an objective commentator on the claims of these political alignments.

427. and both parties were influential...

Boeotian policy from 431-404, and especially during the Decelean war, was consistently and strongly anti-Athenian. After the Spartans had come to terms with Athens in 404 (annoyance at this (Xen. *Hell.*II.2.19) echoed Boeotian refusal to join in the peace of 421: Th.V.2.26) Boeotian anti-Athenianism no longer necessarily implied support of Sparta. P. Cloché ('La politique thébaine de 404 à 396 av. J.-C.' *REG* 31 (1918), pp.315-343) traces the stages by which the anti-Spartan element in Boeotian politics grew in influence.

428. many came forward from the cities in Boeotia...

Hetaereiai, the dining clubs which were also political associations, would normally restrict membership to citizens of the city they existed in. In this case, after about fifty years following the integrated constitution described in 16, the political establishment of Thebes was admitting members from the oligarchic élites of the other Boeotian cities.

430. and even a little while earlier

Cloché (art.cit.p.334) opposes the idea that the Ismenias faction had taken power from 404: his preferred explanation is that the Leontiades faction had compromised its pro-Spartan attitude to keep power. Hence Boeotia's non-participation in Sparta's wars against Elis and Persia: but taking the leading role in an anti-Spartan coalition which included Athens, which Thebes came to do as a result of provoking the Locrian-Phocian war, represented a much more radical position. The attraction of Cloché's view is that it fits in well with the Oxyrhynchus author's statement that both parties in Thebes were influential.

Xenophon (*Hell*. III.5.3) does not supply details of the political position in his version of the story, and simply calls the Androcleidas party 'the leading men in Thebes'. Diodorus omits any reference to the Boeotian government (XIV.81.1-3).

436. when the Spartans were at Deceleia...

In 413 the Spartans established a permanent post in Attica at Deceleia (Th.VII.19.1), up towards the Boeotian border. This put more sustained pressure on the Athenians than they had suffered earlier in the war.

440. because the city was profiting considerably on their account

The Spartan strategy benefitted Boeotia in proportion to the damage it did to Attica. It made moves against Boeotia by the Athenians (like the Delium campaign of 424) much less likely.

443. when the Athenians began to move against Boeotia...

Engrossing these small Boeotian communities into Thebes gave the Thebans the advantage of a larger population, in the city and under the direct control of the government. Later, in Epaminondas' campaigns after Leuctra, the Thebans sponsored synoecism at Messene and Megalopolis (D.S.XV.66.1 and 72.4) - this time with the idea of concentrating Messenian and Arcadian strength against the power of Sparta.

450. they bought up the slaves...

At VII.27.5 Thucydides comments on the damage caused to Attica during the occupation of Deceleia. He mentions that more than 20,000 slaves ran away to Deceleia: the Spartans coped with this influx by selling the slaves locally.

454. the wood and tiles of the houses...

Much of southern Greece was not well wooded even at this date; this is why roof timbers and door frames were worth taking away. Thucydides notes (II.14.1) how at the beginning of the Peloponnesian war the Athenians, obeying Pericles' instructions, brought everything in from the country, including the woodwork of their houses.

455. At that time the Athenians' territory....

The power of Athens was supported by successful agriculture in Attica as well as the league tribute and the output of the silver mines. Depriving

Athens of control of Attica was a necessary part of Sparta's strategy for final victory. The Boeotians were the incidental beneficiaries of the destruction of Attic prosperity.

457. it had suffered only slight damage

In view of the nature of the 'Periclean strategy' - allowing invasions of Attica and relying on control of the sea - it may seem odd that the countryside outside Athens had not been very thoroughly ravaged. But invading armies were only in Attica for a few weeks (until the occupation of Deceleia). Destroying standing crops was easy, but destroying buildings was much more time-consuming. W.G. Hardy, though noting that it is unnecessary to cut down a tree to kill it, points out that two Atthidographers, Androtion (*FGrHist* 324 F 39) and Philochorus (*FGrHist* 328 F 125), say that sacred olive trees were spared in the Archidamian war ('*The Hellenica Oxyrhynchia* and the devastation of Attica' *C.Phil.* 21 (1926), pp.346-355 at p.351).

XVII (Column 14 line 6 to column 15 line 32)

468. wanting to overthrow their empire so that they would not be swept aside...

The author gives his explanation of the beginning of the Phocian-Locrian war in terms of the internal politics of Boeotia. Taking the view that attempting to overthrow the power of Spartans was such a risky enterprise that the Boeotian government, even if controlled by an anti-Spartan faction, cannot have had it in mind, *Bruce,* pp.116-7, suggests that the motive (fear of the pro-Spartan party) may have been imagined by the writer as a result of looking back on the events of 383/2 when the pro-Spartans did betray the Cadmea to a passing Spartan army.

But this suggestion ignores the author's careful stressing of the point that both parties were influential in Thebes. The background filled in in the two previous chapters is structured to support the explanation offered here: nature of the system; even power of the sides; anti-Spartans recently taking power; what the city had gained in the past from friendship with Sparta. The writer's aim has been to make the reader feel he understands the factors which led to the decisions which were made by the people in power. The fact that the anti-Spartans struck first makes it impossible to judge whether their fear of the pro-Spartans was realistic.

470. supposing that the King would provide the money...

Back in 7.2, discussing opposition to Sparta in Athens, the author notes how a number of states, including Boeotia, had for some time been looking for a way to get up an alliance to fight a war against the Spartans. This atmosphere of anti-Spartanism, together with the Persian King's initiative in sending Timocrates to pay out money to get a war started and force Sparta's withdrawal from Asia (Xen. *Hell.* III.5.1-2), created conditions where trying to provoke the Spartans into military action could seem an intelligent course of action for the Ismenias party.

477. they thought it would be difficult to attack them openly...

In an article ('Internal Politics and the Outbreak of the Corinthian War' *Emerita* 28 (1960), pp.75-86), Bruce makes the underhand nature of this provocative action a main point in his argument against accepting the author's account of the beginning of the war. He asks (p.80) whether the reader is to imagine that all, or only some, of the anti-Spartan party knew of the plan. The first alternative he finds implausible; and since the second would involve the leading men deceiving their own supporters (p.81), who might be expected later to feel that their trust had been abused, he thinks it difficult to accept in view of Ismenias' and Androcleidas' success in keeping their prominent position in the anti-Spartan party until 383/2 (cf. Xen. *Hell.* V.2.25-31).

This is not a strong argument. The 'party' was a loose alliance of people of similar opinions, and not a bureaucratically organized unit of politicians who would expect to be consulted. The leaders' success in starting the desired war probably earned admiration rather than annoyance. And the anti-Spartans were right, probably on several counts, to think that an open attack - a march against Sparta - was not a practical plan.

481. they persuaded certain men among the Phocians...

Xenophon (*Hell.* III.5.3) agrees with this author on the point of the Boeotians having provoked the Spartans to attack by underhand action in connection with the Phocian-Locrian dispute. But on nearly all further details the two disagree. It is not only a question of his saying that the Boeotians had made their arrangements with the Locrians, but also of his placing the dispute between Phocis and *Eastern* Locris, while the *Hellenica Oxyrhynchia* places events around Parnassus, on the border between Phocis and Western Locris (see map). Pausanias III.9.9 speaks of the Locrians of Amphissa (Western Locrians) in this connection.

The differences are almost as great as those in the accounts of the Battle of Sardis (see 11 above, with notes); in this case the argument that Xenophon may have been on the spot is not really available. Bruce's suggestion (art. cit. p.85) that the Oxyrhynchus author may have had a pro-Spartan Boeotian informant is speculative. It is the fact that the *Hellenica Oxyrhynchia* account gives a location for the border dispute ('a disputed area near Mt. Parnassus') which conveys the impression that the writer has a clearer knowledge than Xenophon about what was going on.

LOCRIS, PHOCIS and BOEOTIA

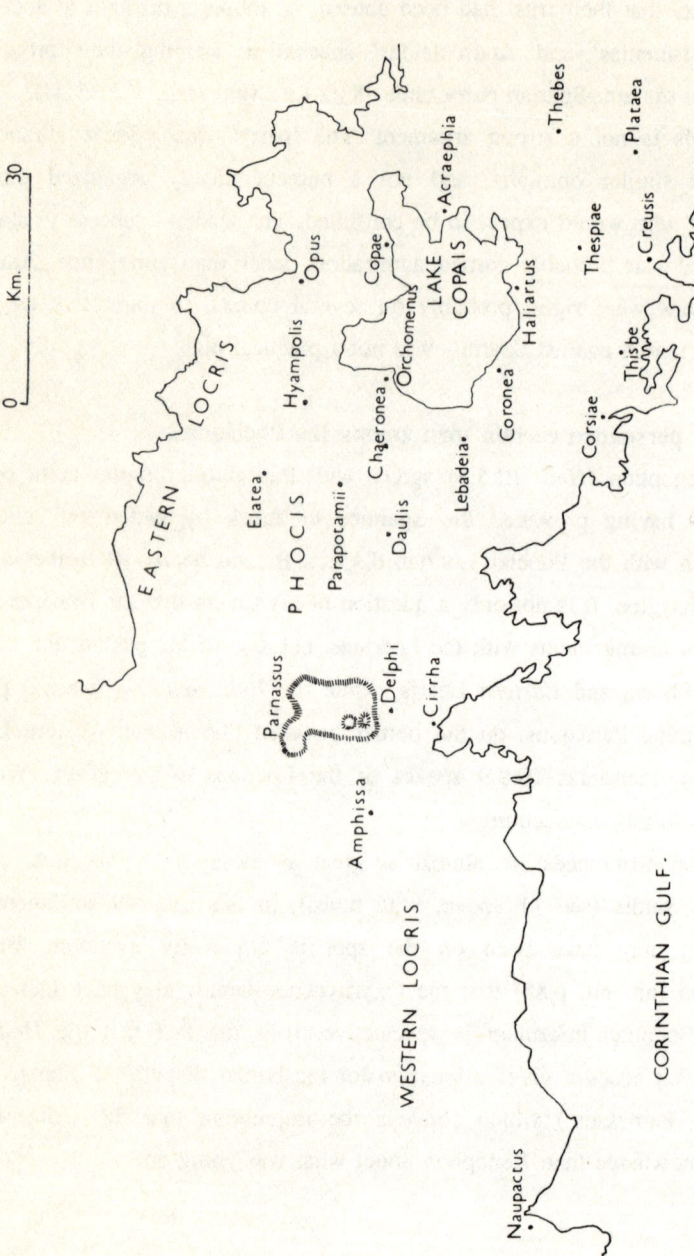

It may be that Xenophon found it more plausible to think of the Boeotians as intriguing with Locrians rather than Phocians; in any case the account of the Oxyrhynchus author is a bit more unexpected, since the Phocians were usually the rivals of the Locrians, who were generally friendly with the Boeotians. The less obvious version probably merits consideration. At the same time the author's general liking for stratagems (see above, notes to 11, p. , and Introduction, p.) may perhaps be reason for scepticism.

K.L. McKay in his article ('The Oxyrhynchus Historian and the Outbreak of the "Corinthian War"' *CR* n.s.3 (1953), pp.6-7) is quite open about preferring on grounds of plausibility the idea of Boeotians paying Locrians, rather than Phocians, to further their policies. He argues that the Locrian reprisal raid was the first unusual move in the border dispute. But in fact the armed Phocian invasion of Locris represented a much steeper escalation of hostilties.

501. the Phocians, when news reached them of events in Thebes...

Xenophon (*Hell*. III.5.4) places the Phocian appeal to Sparta after the Boeotian invasion of Phocis; in this account the Phocians ask for help before the Boeotians invade. Xenophon's account avoids the embarrassment of portraying the Spartans as starting their campaign to support an ally which had been deceived by the Boeotians, but Xenophon does say (*Hell*. III.5.5) that the Spartans were keen to fight the Thebans.

506. told the Boeotians not to make war on the Phocians...

Understandably confused about what was going on, the Spartans sent a message to the Boeotians (not, apparently, the Locrians) which seems to have represented an attempt at not making things any worse. The extant part of Diodorus' account says nothing about the Spartan expedition: the author moves on to another subject after the return home of the Boeotian army.

520. having overrun part of the plain...

Bruce, p.121, takes the fact that the Boeotian army only pillaged the land as evidence that the attack on Phocis was hastily arranged and unpremeditated. This is not convincing: if the anti-Spartan leaders did carry out the stratagem as described, then they would have persuaded their countrymen into action at a late stage. The intention of the leadership was not to capture towns in Phocis; the aim was only to produce a Spartan reaction.

XIX (Column 15 line 32 to column 16 line 29)

The account of the events of 395 continues; the focus switches back to the Asia Minor seaboard. Conon travels inland to Tithraustes to collect money to pay his troops. Diodorus XIV.81.4-6 relates a visit of Conon to Artaxerxes, the King of Persia, in this year. The visit to the King quite likely took place in addition to the visit described in this chapter, since Tithraustes was able to provide only a proportion of the pay that was required. Nepos *Conon* 3.2-4 and Justin VI.2.12-13 suggest that this visit to the King may not have involved Conon's actually entering the royal presence.

530. Now that Cheiricrates had arrived...

The order of Spartan admirals was Pharax, Archelaidas, Pollis, Cheiricrates. Given that the 'eighth year' referred to at 9.1 was 396/5 (see above, pp.137-8), then the chronology would be as follows: 398/7 Pharax, 397/6 Archelaidas, 396/5 Pollis, 395 Cheiricrates.

A complication is introduced by Xenophon, who narrates, after the account of the battle of Sardis and before the sending of Timocrates, how Agesilaus put a person called Peisander in charge of the fleet and at the same time caused 120 new ships to be built (Xen. *Hell.* III.4.29). Peisander died in 394 at the battle of Cnidus. The conclusion that Xenophon's chronology is wrong here is hard to avoid: he mentions Agesilaus' appointment of Peisander before beginning to deal with the Locrian-Phoican war; but the *Hellenica Oxyrhynchia*, which uses a fuller list in constructing the narrative, is more convincing.

538. many months' pay

Isocrates (4(*Panegyricus*).142) comments on how the King kept the soldiers deprived of pay for fifteen months during this campaign.

538. they were paid badly by the generals...

The Persian record for paying irregularly is referred to by Thucydides in connection with the Decelean War (Th.VIII.45.1-2; 83.2-3; 99): in the first of these places Thucydides credits Alcibiades with the suggestion. As W.K. Pritchett shows (*The Greek State at War* I (Berkeley and Los Angeles, 1971), pp.24-25), the balance between pay arrears acting as security against desertion and acting as an incentive to desertion was a fine one.

544. responsibility....lies with the King...

After referring back to the able leadership (*prothumia*) of Cyrus which kept the fleet of the Spartan alliance in commission during the Decelean War, the author presents his analysis of the cause of the irregular payment. Thucydides does not attempt a generalized explanation of this kind in this case. But the Oxyrhynchus author has grasped that the phenomenon originated at the heart of the Persian system, and has identified how enterprises tended to be begun with a small advance of money which was not systematically followed up with the necessary support. Isocrates' highly tendentious diatribe against the Persian system (4(*Panegyricus*).138-156) focuses, though in a different way, on similar weaknesses. It is possible that the mention here of the King is a preliminary to describing Conon's visit to the King: this description would have fallen in the portion of the work now lost. At any rate, at the beginning of section 3 the account returns from generalization to the story of Conon's visit to Tithraustes, and in mentioning Cyrus' able leadership (*prothumia*) the author has certainly given himself something to refer back to in his analysis of Conon's achievement in quelling the mutiny (end of 20).

556. two hundred and twenty talents of silver...

The amount actually owed to the troops can be guessed with some plausibility. If four obols (two thirds of a drachma) a day were due to each man in a hundred ships (the crew of each trireme would be about 200), the amount for fifteen months would be:

$$2/3 \times 200 \times 100 \times 450 = 6{,}000{,}000 \text{ drachmae}$$
$$1{,}000 \text{ talents}$$

but if the daily rate were only 3 obols, the rate before Lysander persuaded Cyrus into granting an increase in 407 (Xen. *Hell.* I.5.6-7), then the total would be correspondingly less. As the narrative shows, there were some land forces to pay as well as the ships' crews. The total required was probably not less than 800 talents, and possibly well over 1000.

558. Tithraustes...went inland to the King...

It is at this point in the narrative that the carefully balanced, almost ring-compositional, nature of chapter 19 becomes noticeable. The remark about Cyrus and the fleet during the Peloponnesian War, half way through the chapter, acts as a pivotal element:

Spartan officer takes up command
Conon journeys to Tithraustes

- the pay owed to Conon's men
- generalization: the usual Persian practice
- how Cyrus saved the fleet
- explanation: the King is personally responsible
- Tithraustes pays out money
- Tithraustes journeys to the King
- Persian officers take up command

The elements identified here occupy slightly differing amounts of space in the chapter but the pattern is clear. And there are other features adding to the force of the author's generalization and explanation: Conon has to visit Tithraustes, and Tithraustes has to visit the King - the impression is given of a ponderous system where the likelihood of obtaining results rests on the hierarchical position of the applicant; and the mention of 700 talents left with Ariaeus and Pasiphernes (though land campaigning had to be paid for as well as the fleet) reinforces the point about grudging payment.

XX (Column 16 line 29 to column 18 line 33)

Columns 17 and 18 are much more fragmentary than columns 11 to 16 or 19 to 21, so that the text is less secure at this point than in most of the latter half of the *Hellenica Oxyrhynchia*.

563. Those of the Cyprians in Conon's forces...

Evagoras, the ruler of Cyprus, had given Conon protection after the defeat of Aegospotami in 404. This Cyprian force was probably provided by Evagoras. Isocrates (9(Evagoras).56) says that Evagoras provided most of the forces which won the naval war against Sparta in 397-394: even if 'most' is an exaggeration, it is fair to assume that these Cyprians (a land force, as the nature of the rumour shows) were part of his contribution.

568. they chose as their general a man of Carpasian race...

Carpasia was a city in Cyprus. Not using this man's name must be regarded as a deliberate move on the writer's part. He could find and use names when he had a particular purpose in mind (see notes to 17, p.162), but here the object is to encourage the reader to think of the mutiny in impersonal terms and treat its leader as a cipher.

It is known from Stephanus of Byzantium (*FGrHist* 115(Theopompus)F19) that Théopompus used the form of ethnic given here (*Karpaseus*, rather than *Karpaseotes*) in book 10 of his *Hellenica*.

575. he negotiated about the matters in hand...

There seems to have been an attempt to settle the mutiny as peacefully as possible. Conon is shown as taking a conciliatory line: here, as in the account of the Rhodian *coup d'état*, Conon appears as a figure who does his best to avoid incurring odium unnecesarily.

586. as he was in the gateway on his way out...

The seizing of the Carpasian by Conon's personal bodyguard without Conon's knowledge led to a fight between them and, first, the Carpasian's own bodyguard, then more of the Cyprian soldiers. This made a tense situation worse: Conon managed to get back inside the city wall, but the Cyprians thought he had been behind the attempt to arrest their leader. Again the author's build-up of Conon as an ideal commander, surrounded through no fault of his own by mutinous doubters and thoughtless loyalists, is carefully augmented.

600. they embarked on the triremes...

Their career in Conon's army over, the Cyprians were planning where to sail. The intention seems to have been to get to Salamis (*Bruce*, p.130, develops the argument for this restoration or Kalinka's) and carry off a *coup d'état* against Evagoras. This was not in theory too far-fetched a proposal - at any rate it was almost exactly the way Evagoras himself had seized power about sixteen years earlier (Isoc. 9 (*Evagoras*).28-32). But after the next damaged portion it becomes clear that either they did not in fact sail away from Caunus, or they soon came to shore again. Bartoletti suggests that they met some difficulty, or were unable to sail the ships.

614. that he was the only one who could save the King's campaign...

Again the author's interest in stratagems comes to the fore. This one is cleverly introduced: what Conon said to the officer in charge of the infantry is reported without explanation of what was behind it. By putting enigmatic statements in Conon's mouth ('he was going to put an end to the disturbance in the camp') the writer is being enigmatic himself.

628. he arrested the Carpasian...

Bruce, p.129, comments on G. Barbieri's observation (*Conone* (Rome, 1955), p.133) of the author's distancing Conon from cruel actions in the case of his bodyguard's attempt at seizing the Carpasian, that 'such reasoning would presumably regard the crucifixion of the Carpasian... as ' wholly justified'. This dismissal of a comment on the author's aims is unfair: the reader is shown the stages by which the mutiny, which begins as a meeting for complaints and which Conon is shown as trying to calm down, eventually passes beyond the point where explanation or discussion could settle it. Although Conon's punishments caused further unrest, this time in Rhodes, the whole tenor of the account is not to treat them as cruel or unusual.

639. on account of Conon and his energy

This recalls Cyrus' *prothumia*, the heart of chapter 19 (see notes to 19

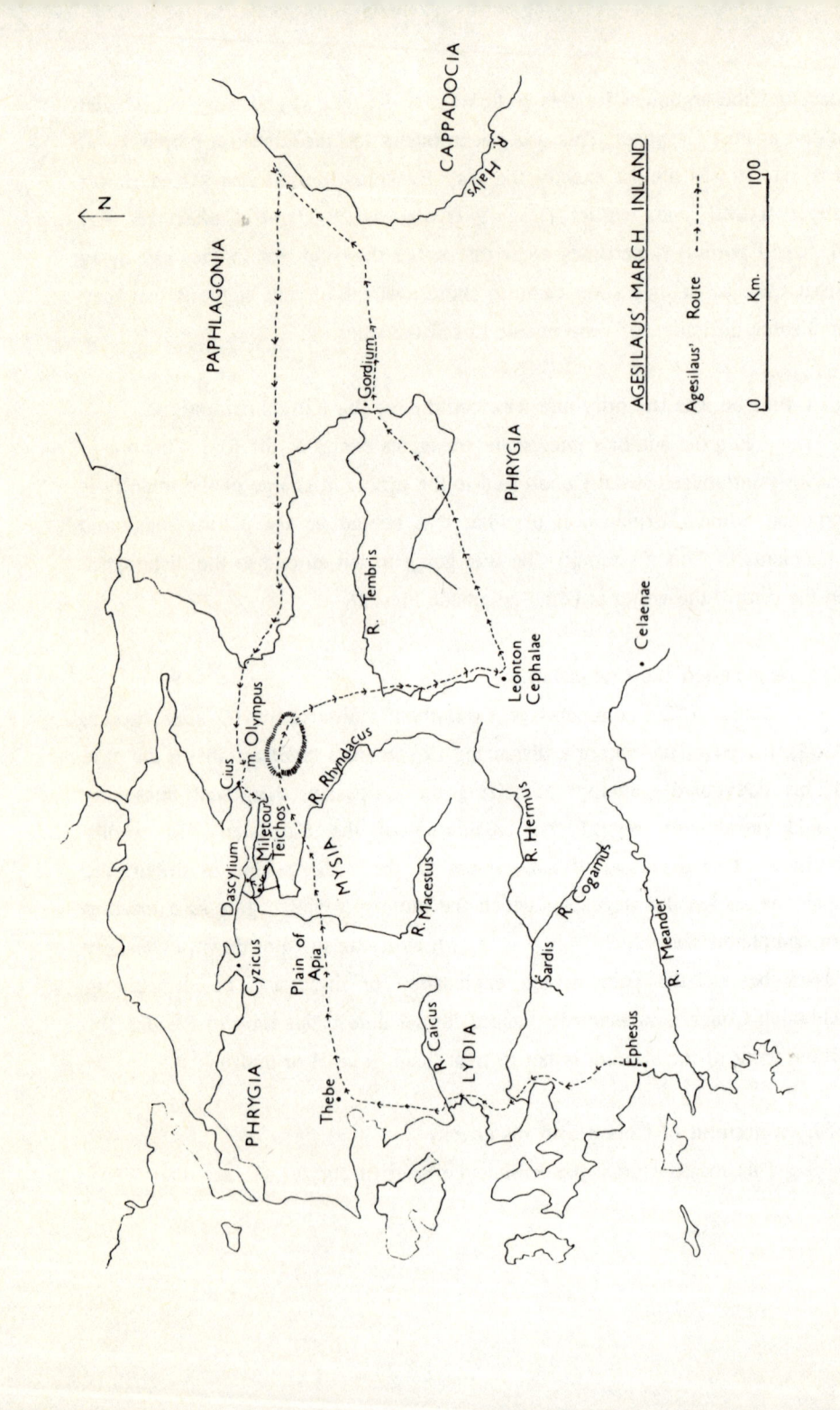

above, p.171).Conon is shown as the new Cyrus, the King's brightest general, the one whose force of personality can mediate between the monolith of Persian power and the frailties of the people who are 'the royal army'. The account of events at Caunus shows his mind at work: subordinates jeopardise a delicate position, but he triumphs by hiding his counsels from friend and enemy alike. In the briefer account of trouble at Rhodes he merely kills the ringleaders and pays the rest: his arrival on the scene brings the power-relations back to normal. Without resort to rhetorical pleading, the author shapes his account to lead the reader to admire Conon.

XXI (Column 18 line 33 to column 20 line 38)

Chapters XXI and XXII deal with the manoeuvres of Agesilaus' army in Asia Minor in the autumn of 395. Xenophon copes with the material differently: after introducing Tithraustes and recording the truce made between him and Agesilaus (*Hell.* III.4.25-26), he notes the army's move into Phrygia then launches on the complexities of the naval command, Timocrates' mission, and the Boeotian-Phocian war. The journey as far as Paphlagonia he copes with in a few lines when he returns to Asia (*Hell.*IV.1.1): then he deals elegantly with the marriage negotiations brought about by Agesilaus between Otys and Spithridates.

The truce was almost certainly introduced in a lost portion of the *Hellenica Oxyrhynchia*: it is mentioned at D.S.XIV.80.8. But the radically different treatments of the two authors are very important from the point of view of Spartan strategy and from the literary point of view. Reading through the accounts of Agesilaus' half hearted attacks on the towns he passes one could wonder what the strategic point of all the marching was. One can see why Xenophon omits it and focuses on personalities - Agesilaus, Otys, Spithridates, later Pharnabazus. D.M. Lewis makes the point that the Spartan army in Asia could reduce the King's revenue and upset the structure of

Persian settlement (*Sparta and Persia* (Leiden, 1977) p.141): this is how pressure was being brought to bear on the Persian government through the Spartans' tactics. The literary side of this bears on the question of authorship: Porphyry had read both Xenophon and Theopompus on the meeting of Agesilaus and Pharnabazus and concluded that Theopompus had changed much of what was in the *Hellenica*, and for the worse (*FGrHist* 115(Theopompus) T21). This has been used as an argument against accepting Theopompus as author of the *Hellenica Oxyrhynchia* - for instance by G.E. Underhill ('Theopompus (or Cratippus), Hellenica' *JHS* 28 (1908), pp.277-290 at p.286).

This argument depends on the assumption that Porphyry could distinguish accurately between a plagiarized account with many changes and an independent contemporary account of the same events (cf. Introduction, p.10).

645. the truce agreed with Tithraustes

D.S. XIV.80.8 explains that the truce was of six months' duration. Here it becomes clear that it applied only in Lydia. Tithraustes had paid thirty talents for this arrangement (Xen. *Hell*.III.4.26).

646. he swooped down into Pharnabazus' country...

The author here picks an uncommon verb. It is used of birds or bees swooping down, and sometimes of ships coming to harbour (cf. *LSJ* s.v. *Katairo*); despite the second of these uses it seems problematic to take it as an exact equivalent to 'he went' (*elthen* or similar). *FGrHist* 115 (Theopompus) F265 notes *katarai* as an equivalent of *elthein* used by Theopompus: yet even if Theopompus' authorship is accepted, partly on the basis of this point of style, it should not necessarily be taken that this usage is a dead metaphor. Cf. note on 13 above.

647. he led the army forward plundering...

See the map for Agesilaus' route: he moves first northwards, and there is a brisk mention of areas he goes through. Keeping Agesilaus as the subject of the sentence, the writer focuses on how the pillage was at the general's direction rather than accidental.

649. Apia, as it is called...

U. von Wilamowitz restored *Apias* here: the place name fits the gap and is known from Strabo XII.1.70 and Polybius V.77.9.

651. For the majority of the Mysians are independent...

The Persian empire used a complex system of control. When the Mysians are described as autonomous, it is not implied that there is no connection with the Persian government: the King proposes via Tithraustes at Xen. *Hell*. III.4.25 that the Spartans should go home and 'that the cities in Asia, being autonomous, should pay him the ancient tribute'. In this case the Mysians were divided on whether to join in action against the Persian government.

658. wanting a safe passage through it...

Bruce (pp.135-136), and before him C. Dugas, raises the question why Agesilaus led his army over Mysian Olympus rather than up the Rhyndacus valley. Probably he did not expect to be attacked; in any case he had not been there before and had no way of knowing exactly what the difficulties would be. A number of incidents on the march illustrate the improvised nature of Agesilaus' tactical decisions. These details would hardly suit Xenophon, who, as Dugas ('La Campagne d'Agésilas en Asie Mineure' *BCH* 34 (1910), pp.58-95 at p.73) notes, was seeking in the *Agesilaus* to provide a 'moral physiognomy' of his hero.

667. he posted in an ambush many of the Dercylidean mercenaries...

These were the soldiers who had campaigned with Cyrus and Xenophon in the famous march on Babylon and the retreat afterwards. They had entered Sparta's service under the command of Thibron (Xen. *Anab.* VII.8.24) and evidently later been named after Thibron's successor Dercylidas (Xen. *Hell.* III.1.8).

Here again the author gives a story of a stratagem (see Introduction above, p. 16): and who better, from the author's point of view, as the chief actors in an ambush, than this famous unit? But equally, Agesilaus would presumably have found them the natural choice for the job under these circumstances.

690. not into the region which he had invaded

This operation in 396 is referred to at D.S.XIV.79.3 and was aimed at Hellespontine Phrygia.

692. Spithridates

Xenophon adds the detail that Spithridates' adhesion to Agesilaus' cause began with Lysander persuading him to revolt against the Persian government (*Hell.* III.4.10): but here the Oxyrhynchus author only alludes in a general way to how this had happened (the historians agree on the rift between Spithridates and Pharnabazus: Xen. *Ages*. 3.3 explains what Spithridates was offended about); and he puts a distancing 'it is said' before the spicy comment about Agesilaus' attraction towards Spithridates' son.

It is worth noticing how there is no general suggestion that Agesilaus was hoping to collect Persian defectors. The support he did gather on the march was from marginal elements in the Persian Empire. In fact, Spithridates too had put himself in a marginalized position by becoming the enemy of Pharnabazus, who was in a much more powerful position in the imperial hierarchy. The best he could expect with magnates who had something to hope for from the King was to neutralize them: Tithraustes had been forced to agree to the truce, and Pharnabazus in the winter of 395/4 promised Agesilaus his support if the King decided to make him subordinate to someone else in the campaign against Sparta (Xen. *Hell.* IV.1.37-38).

707. made attacks on it...

Sieges were not part of Agesilaus' programme. The army was not carrying the equipment that would have been needed to make an attack on a fortified city likely to succeed.

717. Spithridates was urging him to march into Paphlagonia

Xenophon notes (*Hell.* IV.1.2) that Spithridates had undertaken to make the King of the Paphlagonians Agesilaus' ally, and says how Agesilaus had been hoping for a long time to get a nation to revolt from the King. The Oxyrhynchus author does not mention a motive, but the momentum of his narrative makes the move plausible - Agesilaus has to march his army somewhere.

XXII (Column 20 line 38 to column 21 line 39)

722. to Gyes...

Xenophon calls this king Otys in the *Hellenica* (e.g. IV.1.3) and Cotys in the *Agesilaus* (3.4). Thys, the Paphlagonian king in *F.Gr.Hist* 115 (Theopompus) F179, and Thuys, in Nepos *Datames* 2-3, may be other Greek and Latin renderings of the same non-Greek name.

724. Agesilaus made a truce...

The author does not treat the meeting and negotiations as a very important incident. Xenophon by contrast puts them at the heart of a vivid passage with striking use of direct speech (*Hell*.IV.1.3-15) and seeks to give emphasis to the events in his account.

This gives rise to difficulty in judging which version embodies a more accurate assessment of the significance of the events. C. Dugas ('La Campagne d'Agésilas en Asie Mineure' *BCH* 34 (1910), pp.58-95 at pp.84-85) argues that Xenophon has transformed an insignificant fact into an important event: the basis of his argument is the brevity and dryness of the Oxyrhynchus account, which he finds more convincing than Xenophon's literary and dramatic developments. But the *Hellenica Oxyrhynchia* author knew how to use a plain style to suggest and convince.

726. he feared that they would be short of supplies for the winter

Xenophon (*Hell*. IV.1.1) puts the arrival in Phrygia from Lydia in the early autumn: here the Oxyrhynchus author uses a dating reference which suggests that the two writers agree on the chronology of this part of the campaign.

740. River Rhyndacus...Lake Dascylitis...Dascylium

What the reader does not find out here is that Dascylium (Xen. *Hell*. IV.1.15-16) was the site of Pharnabazus' palace. The passage in Xenophon mentions a river flowing by the palace, and this is presumably the River Rhyndacus. Xenophon stresses the amenities available to Agesilaus' soldiers at these winter quarters (and denied to Pharnabazus, Xen. *Hell*. IV.1-25), while this author presents Dascylium as an imperial fortress - which Agesilaus did not take. This last aspect is rather avoided by Xenophon, who blandly mentions the prosperous villages outside the town.

752. pay for the soldiers

C. Dugas (p.89) notes on this and the mention of the Mysians being allowed home for the winter that 'Xenophon neglects these little details which, as they interest the administrator more than the general, add nothing to the glory of the king of Lacedaemon'. The reader naturally also thinks of 19: the author gives attention to how the armies of both sides were maintained.

755. to go...to Cappadocia...

The Spartan army was recalled to Greece before Agesilaus could embark on this expedition: the King's strategy of indirect pressure worked before Agesilaus could force a settlement on the terms the Spartans hoped for. The (mistaken) geographical idea seems to have been that Asia Minor was a kind of triangle tapering away eastwards, so that Sinope (on the Black Sea) would not be far north of Cilicia and the Mediterranean coast.

INDEX

(References to Introduction, Translation and Commentary)

Acraephnium, 83, 156 (Map), 159
Aegean Sea, 17, 18, 20, 133
Aegina, 47, 53
Aegospotami, Battle of, 19, 20, 133, 173
Aeneas Tacticus, 117, 130, 131
Aeschines, 132, 136
Aesimus, 47, 134
Agesilaus, 10, 15, 16, 20, 23, 59, 63, 65, 67, 71, 105, 107, 109, 111, 113, 134, 138, 141, 143–6, 147, 149, 170, 177–8, 179, 180–1, 182, 183
Agis, 118
Alcibiades, 18–19, 125–7, 130, 133, 171
Ambushes, 99, 107, 180
Amorges, 18
Amphipolis, 51, 137
Androcleidas, 85, 89, 91, 161, 163, 167
Androtion The Atthidographer, 13, 165
Antalcidas, Peace of (King's peace), 152, 154
Antiochus, 15, 16 (n.), 41, 126–9
Antitheus, 85, 162
Anytus, 47, 134
Apia, Plain of, 6, 105, 176 (Map)
Apollophanes of Cyzicus, 10
Arcadia, 164
Arcadian League, 153
Archelaidas, 55, 139, 170
Archidamian War, 13, 17, 165
Archinus, 12
Arginusae, Battle of, 20, 116, 122
Argos, 17, 49, 51, 89, 136
Ariaeus, 97, 148, 173
Aristophanes, 132
Aristotle, 13, 122, 153, 155
Arrian, 22
Arsinoite Nome, 4
Artaxerxes II, 19, 148
Artemis, Temple of (Ephesus), 119 (Map), 120
Asia, 17, 18, 19, 20, 116, 118, 125, 137, 141, 148, 166, 177, 179, 183
Asias, 85, 87, 162
Athenaeus, 9
Athene, Treasury of, 118
Athens, 6, 8, 13, 16, 17, 18, 19, 20, 21, 22, 23, 31, 33, 37, 41, 43, 47, 51, 53, 85, 87, 89, 116–166 (*passim*)
Atthidography, 13
Attica, 13, 17, 53, 87, 137, 163, 164, 165
Augustan Period, 119, 121
Aulis, 87

Authorship, 7–14
Babylon, 17, 19, 180
Bias, 14, 133, 134, 161
Black (Pontic) Sea, 18, 115, 183
Boeotarch, 83, 157–9
Boeotia, 17, 20, 49, 51, 87, 89, 91, 93, 95, 135–6, 152, 154, 156 (Map), 156 (Map), 158, 159, 161, 162–3, 164, 165, 166, 167, 169, 170;
(Constitution) 7, 9, 13, 20, 81, 83, 152, 153, 154–5, 157–61
Boeotian–Phocian War, 153
Brasidas, 17
Byzantium, 130, 131
Cadmea The, 83, 161, 165
Cadmus, 161
Cairo Fragments, 3, 4, 6, 8, 9, 16 (n.), 19, 29ff., 116ff., 118
Cappadocia, 115, 176 (Map), 183
Caria, 132, 134, 139 (Map), 141, 142, (Map), 146
Carians, 103
Carpasia, 174
Carpasian, The, 97, 99, 103, 174, 175
Caunus, 55, 79, 81, 95, 97, 103, 105, 133, 134, 139 (Map), 140, 175, 177
Caunian Lake, 55, 139 (Map), 140
Caunian River, 6, 55, 140
Cayster River, 57, 119 (Map), 142 (Map), 143–4, 146
Celaenae, 67, 142 (Map), 147, 148
Cephalus, 23, 49, 135
Chaeronea, 83, 156 (Map), 159
Cheiricrates, 95, 113, 170
Chios, 123, 130
Chorsiae, 159
Cicero, 10
Cilbiani, 119
Cilicia, 55, 115, 134, 183
Cius, 113, 176 (Map)
Clazomenae, 125, 127, 128 (Map)
Clearchus, 131
Cleisthenes, 160
Cnidus, 139 (Map); (Battle) 9, 133, 134, 150, 170
Coeratadas, 85, 162
Coins, 119, 120–1
Colophon, 41, 116
Colossae, 148
Commodus, 5

184

Conon, 16 (n.), 20, 47, 49, 53, 55, 81, 95, 132, 133, 134, 135, 139, 140, 149, 150, 151, 152; (Quells the mutiny) 97, 99, 101, 103, 105, 171–3, 174, 175, 177
Copae, 83, 156 (Map), 159
Copais, Lake, 156 (Map), 157
Coressus, 6, 31, 118
Corinth, 17, 23, 51, 89, 136
Corinthian War, 12–13, 134, 162
Cornelius Nepos, 181
Coronea, 83, 156 (Map), 159; (Battle) 154
Council of Athens, 47, 132–3
Coup d'Etat, 79, 81, 149–50, 151, 155, 174, 175
Cratesippidas, 123, 130
Cratippus, 7, 9, 11–13
Croesus, 120
Cynossema, Battle of, 9, 116, 125
Cypriots, 97, 99, 101, 103
Cyprus, 20, 101, 133, 173, 174
Cyrus the Elder, 16, 149
Cyrus the Younger, 19, 95, 124, 171–2, 173, 175, 177, 180
Cyzicus, 109, 113, 176 (Map); (Battle) 18, 116
Daimachus of Plataea, 13–14
Darius, 124
Dascylitis, Lake, 113, 182
Dascylium, 113, 176 (Map), 182
Dating System, 8, 12, 13, 53, 137–8
Daulis, 93, 168 (Map)
Decelea, 17, 18, 87, 163, 164, 165
Decelean War, 20, 51, 95, 123, 162, 171
Delian League, 149
Delium Campaign, 164
Demaenetus, 23, 47, 53, 132–3, 137, 161
Demeter and Persephone, Temple of (Byzantium), 43, 130
Democracy, 8, 18, 19, 20, 73, 81, 132, 133–4, 136, 138, 149, 150, 152, 161, 162
Demosthenes, 124, 135
Demotic Official Documents, 3, 4
Dercylidas, 180
Dercylideans, 6, 107, 132, 180
Diagorean Family, 81, 151
Differences between the Xenophon/Plutarch and Hell.Ox./Diodorus Traditions, 15, 116, 125–7, 129, 135, 141, 144, 167, 170, 177–8, 182
Digressions, 23, 81–9, 95, 123
Diocles, 116
Diodorus Siculus, 8, 9, 12, 14, 116–83 (*passim*)
Dionysius of Byzantium, 130
Dionysius of Halicarnassus, 11–12, 13, 22, 116, 118
Dorimachus, 79, 151
Egypt, 3, 5, 7, 17, 24

Elatea, 93, 168 (Map)
Elis, 163
Emendations of the Text, 131, 136
Epaminondas, 164
Ephesus, 41, 126, 128 (Map); (Athenian attack on) 19, 31, 33, 116–7, 118, 119 (Map), 120, 121
Ephorus, 8, 13, 14, 24, 125, 151
Epicrates, 23, 49, 135
Erythrae, 83, 87, 158
Eteonicus, 137
Euclides, 138
Euctemon, 116
Eutresis, 83, 156 (Map), 157, 159
Evagoras, 133, 134, 173, 175
Florence Fragments, 4, 6, 8, 9, 19, 35ff., 116, 117, 122ff., 136
Glaucippus, 116
Gordium, 111, 176 (Map)
Gyes, 111, 113, 181
Hagnias, 49
Haliartus, 83, 156 (Map)
Harpocration, 151
Hellenica Oxyrhynchia, *passim*
Hellespont, 105, 113, 126, 133, 180
Hendiadys, 133, 161
Herodotus, 21, 22, 24, 120
Hetaereiai, 163
Hiatus, 6, 24
Hieronymus, 79, 151
Hyampolis, 93
Hyettus (Hysiae), 83, 156 (Map), 157, 158, 159
Hypaepa, 142 (Map), 144
Ismenias, 85, 89, 91, 161, 162, 163, 166, 167
Isocrates, 124, 171, 173, 175
Karabel Pass, 144
Kilbian Plain, 31, 119
Land Fighting, 31, 33, 37, 57, 59, 91, 93, 107, 111, 117–8, 120–1, 141, 143–7
Lebadea, 83, 156 (Map), 159
Leontiades, 85, 87, 161, 163
Leonton Cephalae, 6, 109, 176 (Map)
Leonymus, 101, 103
Leuctra, Battle of, 164
Livy, 24
Locrian–Phocian War, 163, 165, 171, 177
Locris, 91, 93, 167, 168 (Map), 169
London Fragments, 4–5, 6, 7, 9, 20, 23, 45ff., 123, 132ff.
Lucian of Samosata, 22
Lycia, 139 (Map)
Lydia, 17, 65, 67, 105, 116–7, 142 (Map), 178, 182
Lysander, 19, 41, 117, 125–7, 128, 129, 172, 180
Lysias, 6, 7, 116, 118, 135, 155

185

Lysimachus, 119–20
Macedonia, 132
Maeander, River, 65, 67, 141, 147, 148
Magnesia, 71
Media, 17
Megabates, 109, 180
Megalopolis, 164
Megara, 19, 37, 116, 117, 122
Messene, 64
Messenians, 99
Michigan Papyrus, 6, 7
Miletou Teichos, 6, 113, 176 (Map)
Milon, 47, 53
Mutiny, 20, 97, 99, 101, 172, 174
Myndian, 43, 131
Mysia, 16 (n.), 105, 107, 113, 115, 176 (Map), 179, 183
Naupactus, 133
Nicophemus, 79, 151
Nisaea, 122
Notium, 128 (Map); (Battle) 15, 16 (n.), 19, 43, 124, 125–7
Oenophyta, Battle of, 154
Oligarchy, 19, 20, 118, 133, 136, 149, 150, 151, 154–5, 161, 163
Olympic Games, 151
Olympus (Mysian), 6, 105, 113, 176 (Map), 179
Orchomenus, 83, 156 (Map), 157–8, 159, 160
Otys (Gyes), 177, 181
Pactolus River, 141, 142 (Map), 143
Panajir Dagh, 119 (Map), 120
Pancalus, 113
Paphlagonia, 111, 176 (Map), 177, 181
Pasiphernes, 97, 173
Parapotamii, 93, 168 (Map)
Parnassus, Mount, 11, 91, 167 168 (Map)
Pasion (Pasiphon?), 31, 118
Pausanias, 136, 167
Peace of Nicias, 17, 123, 162
Peace Treaties, 17, 18, 123, 134
Pedaritus, 123–4
Pedieis, 93
Peloponnesians, 63, 105, 111, 132, 134
Peloponnesian War, 17–19, 20, 87, 135, 138, 153, 164, 172
Pericles, 164, 165
Persia, 11, 16, 17, 18, 19, 20, 63, 89, 109, 111, 116, 124, 132, 133, 134, 135, 136, 140, 141, 143–5, 146–7, 150, 153, 163, 166, 171, 173, 177, 178, 179, 180
Phanotis, 93
Pharax, 49, 132, 138, 140, 170
Pharnabazus, 10, 51, 55, 95, 105, 109, 113, 177–8, 180–1, 182
Philochorus, 165

Phocaea, 126
Phocis, 11, 81, 91, 93, 95, 153, 163, 167, 168 (Map), 169, 170
Phoebidas, 161
Phoenicia, 20, 55, 115, 134, 139
Photius, 9
Phrygia, 15, 65, 67, 109, 111, 113, 142 (Map), 147, 176 (Map), 177, 180, 182
Phyle, 133
Pindar, 151
Piraeus, The, 19, 47, 132, 134, 135, 137
Pisander, 134, 170
Plataea, 83, 117, 152, 156 (Map), 157–8
Plato Comicus, 135
Pliny the Elder, 119
Plutarch, 8, 12, 22, 124, 125–6, 129, 130
Political Parties, 47–51, 79, 85–9, 135, 149–50, 154, 161–3, 165–7
Pollis, 55, 139, 140
Polyaenus, 135, 148
Polyanthes, 136
Polybius, 10, 15, 22, 179
Porphyry, 10, 13, 178
Possicrates, 4, 31, 33, 120
Potniae, 87
Priene, 67, 142 (Map), 147
Pygela, 116
Pylos, 17, 37, 116, 123, 134
Raids, 91, 116–7, 167
Restorations of the Text, 119, 121, 123, 124, 125, 146, 179
Rhathanes, 111
Rhodes, 16 (n.), 95, 101, 103, 133, 134, 139 (Map), 175, 177; (Coup d'Etat) 79, 81, 149, 150, 151, 153, 174
Rhyndacus, River, 113, 176 (Map), 179, 182
Sacred War, 11
Salamis (Cyprian), 134, 174
Samos, 18, 116, 118, 126–7
Sangarion, River, 113
Sardis, 15–16, 97, 124, 153, 170, 172; (Battle) 65, 141, 142 (Map), 143–6, 147, 167
Scaphae, 83, 87, 158
Scolus, 83, 87, 158
Schoenus, 87
Scholia, 136
Sea–Battles, 18, 19, 20, 41–3, 51–3, 116, 125–7
Sicily, 17, 18, 122, 125, 129
Sidonian Ruler, 55, 139
Simichus, 51, 136
Sinope, 115, 183
Sipylus, Mount, 142 (Map), 143
Socrates, 134
Sparta, 6, 8, 13, 16 (n.), 17, 18, 19, 20, 21, 23, 31, 37, 41, 43, 47, 49, 51, 55, 63, 85, 87,

89, 91, 93, 95, 116–83 (*passim*)
Spithradates, 109, 111, 177, 180, 181
Stephanus of Byzantium, 174
Strabo, 120, 179
Stratagems, 14, 16 (n.), 145, 169, 175, 180
Style And Mannerisms, 6, 23–4, 123, 133, 151, 152, 161
Tanagra, 83, 156 (Map), 158, 159
Telesegorus, 49
Thasos, 51, 130, 137
Thebe, Plain of, 105, 176 (Map)
Thebes, 16 (n.), 81, 83, 85, 87, 89, 91, 93, 117, 133, 152, 154, 156 (Map), 158–9, 160, 161, 163, 164, 166, 168 (Map), 169
Theopompus, 7, 9–11, 12, 14, 24, 174, 178
Theramenes, 6–7, 134
Thespiae, 83, 156 (Map), 157–8, 159, 160
Thibron, 19, 180
Thirty, The, 19, 22, 133–4, 138
Thisbae, 83, 156 (Map), 157, 159
Thoricus, 53, 137

Thrace, 17, 132
Thrasybulus, 118, 126, 130
Thrasybulus, Son of Lycus, 47, 133–4
Thrasyllus, 31, 116–8
Thucydides, 8, 9, 11, 12, 17, 21, 22, 24, 117, 118, 123, 124, 132, 135, 137, 138, 147, 153, 154, 155, 157, 158, 163, 164, 171
Thybarnae, 142 (Map), 143, 145
Timarchus, 31, 33, 120
Timocrates, 49, 135, 166, 170, 177
Timolaus, 23, 51, 136, 137
Tissaphernes, 18, 19, 23, 59, 65, 97, 116, 141, 143–4, 146, 147, 148, 149, 153
Tithraustes, 95, 97, 105, 135, 148, 149, 153, 172–3, 179, 181
Trophies, 37, 43, 65, 126
Truces, 10, 37, 65, 107, 111, 177, 182
Upper Classes, 14, 47, 133, 134, 161
Vivid Narrative, 151, 152
Xenocles, 63, 143, 144
Xenophon, 6–24 (*passim*), 116–83 (*passim*)

Other Greek texts in this series include:

Aeschylus	*Eumenides* ed. A.J. Podlecki *(1989)*
Aristophanes	*Acharnians* ed. A.H. Sommerstein
	Birds
	Clouds
	Knights
	Peace
	Wasps
Dio Cassius	*Roman History Book 53.1–55.9* ed. J.W. Rich *(1989)*
Euripides	*Alcestis* ed D. Conacher
	Electra ed. M. J. Cropp
	Orestes ed. M.L. West
	Phoenician Women ed. Elizabeth Craik
	Trojan Women ed. Shirley Barlow
Greek Orators I	*Antiphon, Lycias* ed, M. Edwards & S.J. Kern
Hellenica Oxyrhinchia ed. P.R. Mckechnie & S.J. Kern	
Menander	*Samia* ed. D.M. Bain
Plato	*Meno* ed. R.W. Sharples
	Phaedrus ed. C.J. Rowe
Plutarch	*Life of Cicero* ed. J.L. Moles *(1989)*
	Lives of Aristeides and Cato ed. D. Sansone *(1989)*
Sophocles	*Antigone* ed. A.L. Brown
Thucydides	*History 2* ed. P.J. Rhodes
	Pylos 425 B.C. ed. J. Wilson

Other Latin texts in this series include:

Cicero	*Philippics II* ed. W.K. Lacey
	Tusculan Disputations I ed. A.E. Douglas
	Verrines II,1 ed. T.N. Mitchell
Joseph of Exeter	*The Trojan War I–III* ed. A.K. Bate
Lucan	*Civil War VIII* ed R. Mayer
Lucretius	*De Rerum Natura IV* ed. J. Godwin
Ovid	*Metamorphoses I–IV* ed. D.E. Hill
Persius	*The Satires* ed. J.R. Jenkinson
Plautus	*Bacchides* ed. J.A. Barsby
Anon.	*The Ruodlieb* ed. C.W. Grocock
Seneca	*Letters: a selection* ed. C.D.N. Costa
Tacitus	*Annals IV* ed. D.C.A. Shotter *(1989)*
Terence	*The Brothers* ed. A.S. Gratwick
	The Self-Tormentor ed. A.J. Brothers
Virgil	*Aeneid Book VI* ed. F.M. Ahl *(1989)*
William of Newburgh	*The History of English Affairs* ed. P.G. Walsh & M. Kennedy